ILLUSTRATED QUICKEN

Douglas Warwick

David Fulton Publishers
London

David Fulton Publishers Ltd
2 Barbon Close, London WC1N 3JX

First published in Great Britain by
David Fulton Publishers 1993

British Library Cataloguing in Publication Data

A catalogue record for this book is available from the British Library

ISBN 1-85346-269-1

Trademarks mentioned in this book belong, as indicated, to the following organisations:

IBM Corporation: IBM
Microsoft Corporation: Windows
Intuit Ltd.: Quicken, Billminder

Designed by Almac Ltd., London
Typeset by RGM Associates, Southport
Printed in Great Britain

Contents

Getting Started

Introduction

Intuit Quicken, though new to the United Kingdom, claims to be the world's best selling personal and small business financial software package, with over 3 million copies sold in the USA since 1984. Adapted comprehensively to meet UK requirements for such items as SERPS, TESSAs and VAT, version 6 for DOS was very successfully introduced to the UK market in the autumn of 1992; in the spring of 1993 Quicken UK version 2 for Windows followed. The Windows version is the one used in the main part of this guide: the installation and setting up of Quicken for DOS is covered in an appendix.

While users of Quicken can look forward to great savings in time and worry, these will only be achieved if the business of keeping accounts is undertaken in a disciplined way. If care is taken to see that all transactions are promptly and accurately entered, however, the rewards are considerable: not the least of which is a feeling of satisfaction.

Minimum Hardware Requirements

Quicken for Windows requires an IBM or compatible 286 or higher computer with 2MB RAM, one floppy drive, a hard disk with 3MB available, Windows version 3.1 and a printer supported by Windows 3.1.

Installation

- Switch on your computer, and if it does not start in Windows, when the C:〉 prompt appears type 〈**WIN**〉 and press the **Enter** key.
- Place Quicken Disk 1 – the Install disk – in floppy drive A. If the Windows Program Manager is not open, **[Dbl-Clk]** on its icon.
- Place the Mouse arrow on **[File]** and **[Clk]** to open the menu. Point to [Run] and **[Clk]** to open the [Run] window.
- **[Clk]** in the [Command Line] box, then type 〈**a:install**〉 and **[Clk]** on [OK].
- When the Quicken Install window opens, **[Clk]** on the [Install] button for express installation using the predefined settings shown in the install options at the foot of the screen.
- **[Clk]** on [OK] when Quicken has been successfully installed. Remove the Quicken master disk and store it in a secure place.
- To run Quicken, **[Dbl-Clk]** on the Quicken group icon to open it, then **[Dbl-Clk]** on the Quicken program icon to start the program.

Conventions

Throughout this guide, the following conventions have been used:

[Clk]	Click the Left Mouse button once
[Dbl-Clk]	Click the Left button twice – quickly
〈**..words..**〉	Type the words between the angled brackets
[File]	Menus are in bold type
[Move]	Menu items and other options

Getting Started

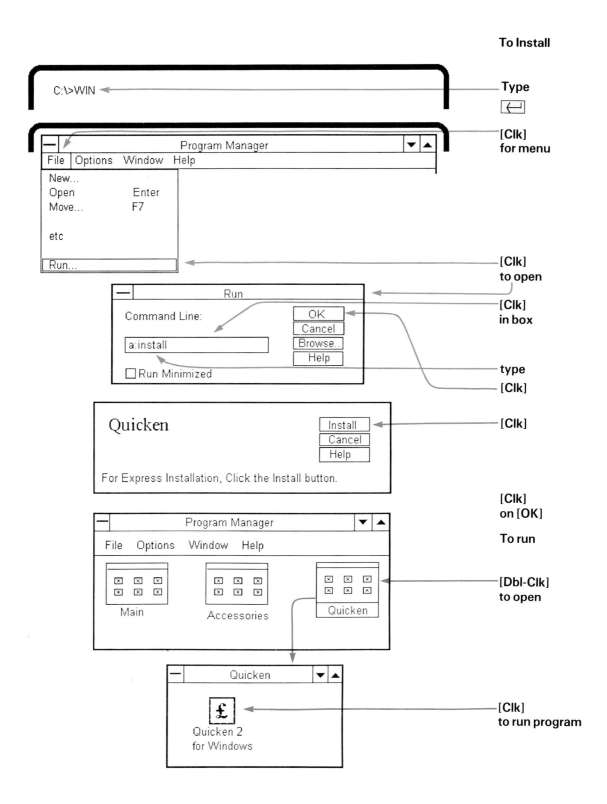

To Install

C:\>WIN

Type
⏎

[Clk]
for menu

Program Manager

File | Options | Window | Help

New...
Open   Enter
Move...   F7

etc

Run...

[Clk]
to open

Run

Command Line: OK
                         Cancel
a:install   Browse..
                         Help
☐ Run Minimized

[Clk]
in box

type
[Clk]

Quicken   Install
                         Cancel
                         Help

For Express Installation, Click the Install button.

[Clk]

[Clk]
on [OK]

To run

Program Manager

File   Options   Window   Help

Main   Accessories   Quicken

[Dbl-Clk]
to open

Quicken

£

Quicken 2
for Windows

[Clk]
to run program

Setting Up

When you start Quicken for the first time, you will be asked first if you wish to see the Windows Tutorial, then if you wish to see the Quicken Tutorial. New users should certainly opt for the "Quick tour" before continuing, but these tutorials may be viewed at any time by choosing [Tutorials] from the **[Help]** menu. After you have seen the tutorials, or clicked on [NO], the First Time Setup window will open.

Instructions

- The First Time Setup window enables you to choose the type of categories Quicken will use to classify your income and expenditure. The default is [Home]. **[Clk]** on the button below to select [Business Categories Only], for the examples in this guide, then **[Clk]** on [OK].
- The Select Account Type window will replace the First Time Setup window. **[Clk]** on [OK] to accept the default [Bank Account].
- Type the information shown in the third frame on the facing page in the appropriate boxes. **[Clk]** on [OK] when you have finished.
- Quicken will show the Transaction Register for this account, with the opening balance posted and marked cleared in the [Clr] field.
- During installation, Quicken has also created a file, "QDATA", to hold the information you put in to the program. You will see this in the title bar at the top of your screen.

Helpful tips

If you have data on an earlier version of Quicken, **[Clk]** on [Cancel] at the First Time Setup window; **[Clk]** on **[File]**, then **[Clk]** on [Open] to use your existing file.

You will need to create a new file to hold the information relating to your own accounts, reserving QDATA for the examples in this guide and for any additional practice you may feel is necessary.

If you need help at any stage, **[Clk]** the **[?]** on the Qcard to see help for that topic, or **[Clk]** on the book to obtain a User Manual page number. **[Clk]** on [Help] in the icon bar to get help on the current window.

Once you have a Help window on your screen, you can view pop up definitions, pursue links with related topics, **[Clk]** [Contents] to see a list of topics, use [Search] to seek information on a specific topic.

As you use this guide, simply follow the step by step instructions; these are supplemented by the illustrations. Add examples of your own, and try out your own ideas. It is hoped that when you reach the end you will be familiar with the basic principles and concepts of Quicken, and ready to apply them to your own circumstances.

To leave Quicken **[Dbl-Clk]** on the Control-menu box in the top left corner of the Quicken window. Quicken will automatically save your work.

Setting Up

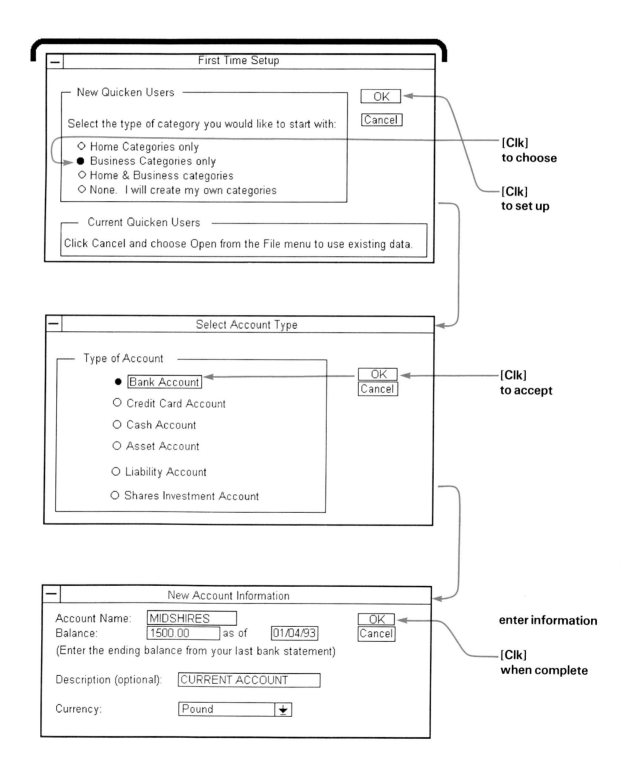

First Time Setup

— New Quicken Users —

Select the type of category you would like to start with:

OK

Cancel

○ Home Categories only
● Business Categories only
○ Home & Business categories
○ None. I will create my own categories

— Current Quicken Users —

Click Cancel and choose Open from the File menu to use existing data.

[Clk]
to choose

[Clk]
to set up

Select Account Type

— Type of Account —

● Bank Account

○ Credit Card Account

○ Cash Account

○ Asset Account

○ Liability Account

○ Shares Investment Account

OK
Cancel

[Clk]
to accept

New Account Information

Account Name: MIDSHIRES
Balance: 1500.00 as of 01/04/93
(Enter the ending balance from your last bank statement)

Description (optional): CURRENT ACCOUNT

Currency: Pound ▼

OK
Cancel

enter information

[Clk]
when complete

Organising

Many users will find the standard categories meet most of their needs, though they may wish to modify the list: you may delete a category if you do not expect to use it and you may add new categories or subcategories, or alter entries in the Category & Transfer List at any time.

Instructions

- **[Dbl-Clk]** the Quicken program icon to start; after the title screen the default QDATA file will open and the menu bar, the icon bar and the bank account Transaction Register will appear – with a helpful "Qcard".

Deleting a Category

- Place the Mouse pointer on [CatList] in the icon bar and **[Clk]** to open the Category & Transfer List.
- Select the category you wish to delete – for example Rental Income – with the Mouse pointer and **[Clk]**.
- Point to the Command Button [Del] and **[Clk][Clk]** on [OK] to confirm the deletion.

Adding a Category

- **[Clk]** on the [New] button to open the [Set Up Category] box.
- Type the name of the new category ⟨**Payroll**⟩ and press **[Tab]** to move to the Description field. Type ⟨**Wages & Salaries**⟩.
- **[Clk]** on the [Expense] option button; **[Clk]** on the [Tax related] check box to select it; **[Clk]** on the arrow to the right of the [Usual VAT Code] frame to open the drop-down list; **[Drag]** the scroll button until "E" appears.
- **[Clk]** on [E] to specify Exempt as the usual VAT code. **[Clk]** on [OK] to set up the new category.

Adding a Subcategory

- **[Clk]** on [New]; type the name and description of the subcategory; **[Clk]** on the [Subcategory of] button. **[Clk]** on the arrow to see the dropdown list. **[Clk]** on [Sales] to select it as the parent category.
- **[Clk]** the [Tax related] check box, and select [Z] as the [Usual VAT Code]. **[Clk]** on [OK] to set up the new subcategory.
- Create the following subcategories of Sales; S4001, Petfoods; S4002, Veterinary Supplies; S4005, Other Sales. Create a subcategory of S4005, S4005Zero for zero rated Other Sales (S4005 will be the parent).
- Create corresponding categories and subcategories under Purchases – P5000.

Helpful tips

The category name [Payroll] is obligatory if you intend to use Quicken to carry out payroll tasks.

Organising

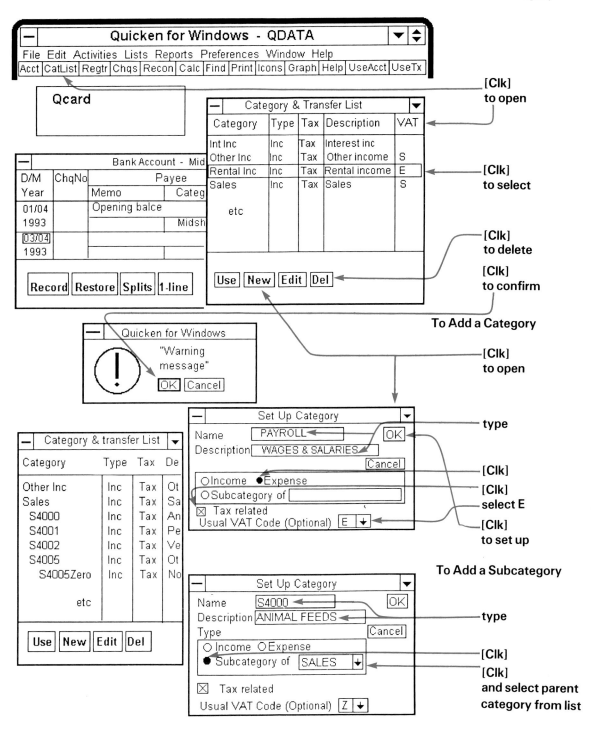

To Delete a Category

Quicken for Windows - QDATA

File Edit Activities Lists Reports Preferences Window Help

| Acct | CatList | Regtr | Chqs | Recon | Calc | Find | Print | Icons | Graph | Help | UseAcct | UseTx |

[Clk] to open

Qcard

Category & Transfer List

Category	Type	Tax	Description	VAT
Int Inc	Inc	Tax	Interest inc	
Other Inc	Inc	Tax	Other income	S
Rental Inc	Inc	Tax	Rental income	E
Sales	Inc	Tax	Sales	S
etc				

[Clk] to select

Bank Account - Mid

D/M Year	ChqNo	Payee / Memo	Categ
01/04 1993		Opening balce	Midsh
03/04 1993			

| Record | Restore | Splits | 1-line |

| Use | New | Edit | Del |

[Clk] to delete

[Clk] to confirm

To Add a Category

[Clk] to open

Quicken for Windows

"Warning message"

| OK | Cancel |

Set Up Category

Name PAYROLL   OK
Description WAGES & SALARIES
Cancel

○Income ●Expense
○Subcategory of [   ]
☒ Tax related
Usual VAT Code (Optional) [E ▼]

type

[Clk]

[Clk] select E

[Clk] to set up

Category & transfer List

Category	Type	Tax	De
Other Inc	Inc	Tax	Ot
Sales	Inc	Tax	Sa
S4000	Inc	Tax	An
S4001	Inc	Tax	Pe
S4002	Inc	Tax	Ve
S4005	Inc	Tax	Ot
S4005Zero	Inc	Tax	No
etc			

| Use | New | Edit | Del |

To Add a Subcategory

Set Up Category

Name S4000   OK
Description ANIMAL FEEDS
Type   Cancel

○ Income ○ Expense
● Subcategory of [SALES ▼]

☒ Tax related
Usual VAT Code (Optional) [Z ▼]

type

[Clk]

[Clk] and select parent category from list

7

Entering Information

When you start Quicken, the opening screen shows the transaction register of the account you created. The register, which resembles a bank statement is, except when you make out cheques at the Write Cheques window (these are entered automatically by the program) where you enter details of your financial activities. Each account that you set up has its own register, and when you record a transaction it is placed in the register firstly in date order, and then, within date order, by cheque number. Quicken then recalculates all balances.

Instructions

- In the register, "today's" date in the empty transaction space after the last entry is highlighted. The flashing cursor is also in this field.
- To move to the next field, press **[Tab]** – or **[Clk]** in the [ChqNo] field. A drop-down list will suggest possible entries. **[Clk]** on [Deposit].
- Type the details shown in the illustration in the [Payee], [Deposit] and [Memo] fields, pressing **[Tab]** to move on as you complete each field.
- Like the [Memo] field, the [Category] field is optional, but classifying transactions is such an important part of controlling your finances that this field should be left blank only in exceptional circumstances.
- If the transaction relates to only one category, **[Clk]** on the arrow in the [Category] field to open the drop-down list, **[Clk]** on the appropriate category to select it and insert it in the field.
- If a transaction covers several categories, you should apportion the total between them. **[Clk]** on the [Splits] button and enter the details shown in the illustration. The Splits total and the Transaction total should agree.
- **[Clk]** on [OK] to close the Splits window and return to the register. The [Category] field shows the word "Splits".
- **[Clk]** on [Record] and Quicken will record and memorise the split transaction. To review it, **[Clk]** in the transaction to select it, if necessary, then **[Clk]** on the [Splits] button – or **[Dbl-Clk]** on the word in the [Category] field.

Helpful tips

If you select Business Categories at installation, Quicken assumes you will wish VAT tracking to be ON. When you first enter a transaction with VAT, you will be asked to confirm the VAT rates: **[Clk]** on [OK] to accept the standard UK VAT rates.

If you know only the gross amount, Quicken will apportion it between net and VAT. Enter the gross in the [Net Amount] column, then **[Clk]** the [Split VAT] button.

If you are not registered for VAT, you may turn off VAT tracking: **[Clk]** on [Preferences] in the Menu Bar, then on [International] and finally on [Use Value Added Tax] check box.

Entering Information

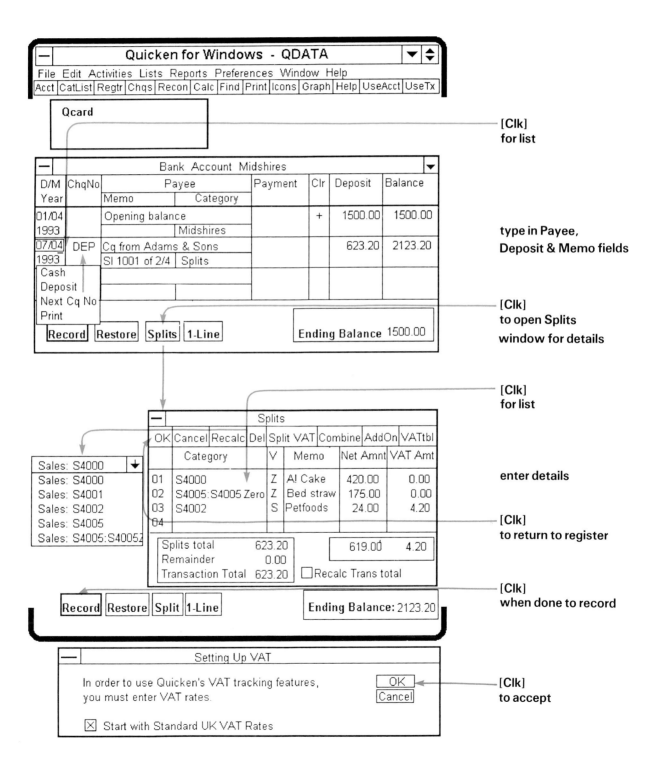

		Quicken for Windows - QDATA				▼	⬍

File Edit Activities Lists Reports Preferences Window Help

Acct | CatList | Regtr | Chqs | Recon | Calc | Find | Print | Icons | Graph | Help | UseAcct | UseTx

Qcard

[Clk]
for list

Bank Account Midshires

D/M Year	ChqNo	Payee		Payment	Clr	Deposit	Balance
		Memo	Category				
01/04 1993		Opening balance			+	1500.00	1500.00
			Midshires				
07/04 1993	DEP	Cq from Adams & Sons				623.20	2123.20
		SI 1001 of 2/4	Splits				

Cash
Deposit
Next Cq No
Print

type in Payee,
Deposit & Memo fields

Record | Restore | Splits | 1-Line

Ending Balance 1500.00

[Clk]
to open Splits
window for details

[Clk]
for list

Splits

OK	Cancel	Recalc	Del	Split VAT	Combine	AddOn	VATtbl

	Category	V	Memo	Net Amnt	VAT Amt
01	S4000	Z	A! Cake	420.00	0.00
02	S4005:S4005 Zero	Z	Bed straw	175.00	0.00
03	S4002	S	Petfoods	24.00	4.20
04					

Sales: S4000	▼
Sales: S4000	
Sales: S4001	
Sales: S4002	
Sales: S4005	
Sales: S4005:S4005	

enter details

[Clk]
to return to register

Splits total	623.20		619.00	4.20
Remainder	0.00			
Transaction Total	623.20	☐ Recalc Trans total		

Record | Restore | Split | 1-Line

Ending Balance: 2123.20

[Clk]
when done to record

Setting Up VAT

In order to use Quicken's VAT tracking features,
you must enter VAT rates.

OK
Cancel

☒ Start with Standard UK VAT Rates

[Clk]
to accept

Writing Cheques

The transaction register is used for all transactions except "Intuit" cheques that are printed from Quicken. When you issue a handwritten cheque the details must be recorded in the register.

Instructions

Handwritten cheques

- If you have more than one bank account, make sure that the one you wish to post the cheques to is open. Have your cheque counterfoils to hand.
- **[Clk]** on the [ChqNo] field. Type in the number of the first cheque you enter in Quicken; for subsequent cheques, **[Clk]** on [Next Chq No] in the drop-down list. (If you do this for the first cheque, Quicken will enter "101".)
- Enter the other details – payee, payment and memo; at the [Category] field, if you enter a category which has a VAT code, the [Splits] window will open. **[Clk]** on [OK] to return to the register, then **[Clk]** the [Record] button to record and memorise the transaction. Home users who wish to split a payment between categories should **[Clk]** on the [Splits] button.

"Intuit" cheques

- **[Clk]** on [Cheques] in the icon bar to open the [Write Cheques] window.
- Press **[Tab]** to accept "today's" date. Enter the payee's name, the amount in figures – Quicken will complete the amount in words – the payee's name and address in the Address box and a memo if desired.
- The [Category] field and the [Splits] window (if required) are completed in the same way as in the transaction register.
- When you have finished, **[Clk]** on [OK] to close the [Splits] window and on the [Record] button to record and memorise the transaction.
- Note the new [Ending Balance] at the bottom of your screen, and the item [Cheques to Print].

Helpful tips

"Intuit" cheques are pre-numbered, and Quicken will enter the correct number in the register when the cheque is printed; there is, therefore, no [ChqNo] field in the [Write Cheques] window.

You may add an extra message line to your cheque – alongside the address box. **[Clk]** on [Preferences], select [Cheques..]; **[Clk]** on the first checkbox, then on [OK].

You can review unprinted cheques by scrolling through the [Write Cheques] window, or by using the transaction register; printed cheques must be examined in the transaction register, where unprinted cheques are distinguished by having "Print" in the [ChqNo] field in place of the number.

Writing Cheques

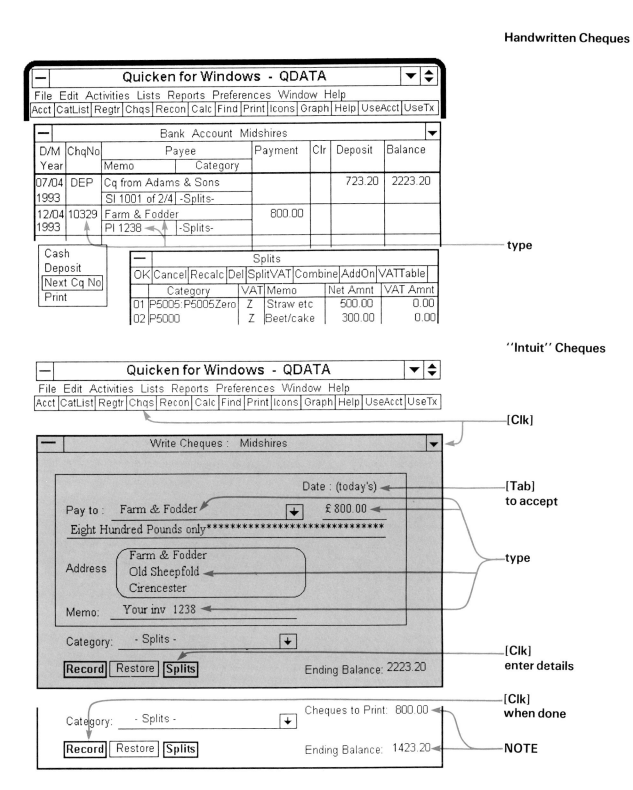

11

Purchases on Credit

If you use "Intuit" cheques, as bills or invoices are received from firms that have supplied you with goods, you can write post-dated cheques, relying on Quicken's "Billminder" and "Reminder" to ensure that the cheques are printed in time to make payments that will benefit from discounts, or escape penalties for late settlement. By entering your liabilities in this way, not only is there less likelihood of a bill being overlooked, but you can also foresee cash requirements over the next few weeks.

Instructions

- Prepare the invoices for entry: first write on them the categories involved and the date payment is due. You may also wish to note your order number on the invoice. The invoices should then be put in order by date due.
- Cheques can then be written directly from the invoice, or from a daybook of bills received. Home users will probably prefer to write their cheques from the bills.
- [Clk] on [Cheques] in the icon bar, and when the [Write Cheques] window opens, alter "today's" date to the date when payment is due. In the example, press [h] for the last day of the current month.
- Complete the cheque in the normal way and [Clk] on [Record] when you have finished. The third illustration shows how Quicken would handle the cheque to Farm & Fodder if it had been post-dated.
- In the transaction register post-dated cheques are separated from other transactions by a bold line, and a Current Balance is given (which does not include post-dated transactions) as well as the Ending Balance (which includes all transactions entered in the register).
- From the summaries in the Bills Received Day Book, write post-dated cheques to pay the other invoices from suppliers.

Helpful tips

If you wish to rapidly scan the entries in a transaction register, [Clk] on the [1-line] button. This will condense each entry to one line; to return to the default two line display, [Clk] on the [2-line] button.

When you begin typing a name in the [Category] field, Quicken will fill in the name for you: if the first few letters fit more than one category, Quickfill completes the first name in the Category List that matches; keep typing until the category you want appears.

Quicken menus may be opened from the keyboard: hold down the [Alt] key and press the key for the letter underlined in the menu you wish to use. Press [Alt+F] to open the [File] menu. Once the menu is open, press the key for the letter underlined in the item you wish to choose. Press [B] to select [Backup] from the [File] menu, for example.

There are also a number of keyboard shortcuts and "Quick Keys"; these are conveniently listed on the back cover of the User Manual.

Purchases on Credit

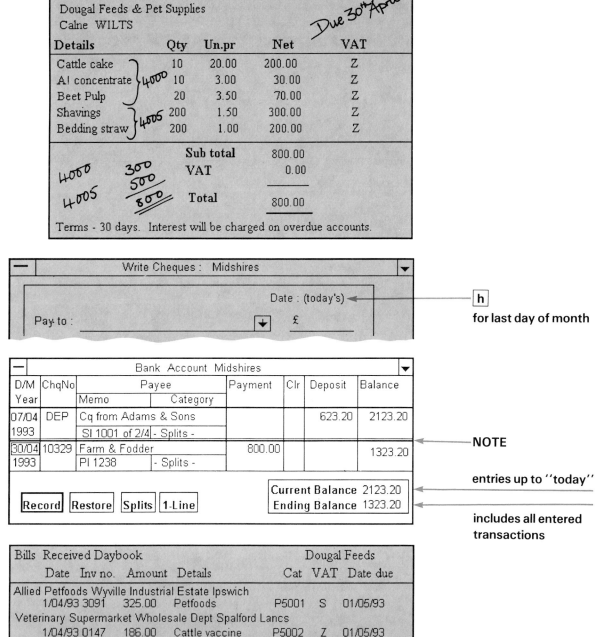

Errors & Adjustments

While a keyboard error can easily be corrected before an entry is recorded in the accounts – simply overtype, pressing **[Shift+Tab]** (hold down one of the Shift keys while pressing Tab) if you need to move back to an earlier field, once an error has been recorded in the transaction register care is needed, especially if you intend to delete an entry, though alterations are not difficult. Once you have a large number of entries in the register, locating a particular transaction is made easy, even if you only possess limited information, by using Quicken's find command.

Instructions

Finding a transaction

- **[Clk]** on [Find] in the icon bar: the find window will open.
- Type ⟨**Adam**⟩ in the Find box, move to the [Search] box and from the drop-down list **[Clk]** on [Payee]. Leave [Contains] in the [Match if] box. Quicken will search the Payee field for entries which contain the word "Adam".
- If you are working at the end of the register, **[Clk]** on [Previous] to search backward, towards the beginning of the register. If the first entry found is not the one you seek, **[Clk]** on [Previous] again. **[Dbl-Clk]** on the [Control-Menu] button to close the [Find] window when the search is done.

Corrections

- **[Clk]** on [Splits] to open the window and **[Clk]** in the second line [Net Amount] field to make it active. Type the correct sum ⟨**275.00**⟩ over the error.
- **[Clk]** in the [Category] field on line 3: the drop-down list will open. **[Clk]** on [S4001] to select it in place of the incorrect category.
- As the correction affects the transaction total, **[Clk]** the [Recalculate Transaction Total] check box before you **[Clk]** on [OK] to leave the [Splits] window. **[Clk]** on [Record] to complete the process.

Deleting

- To delete a transaction, select the transaction, **[Clk]** on [Edit] to open the menu, then on [Delete Transaction]. You will be asked to confirm the deletion, which cannot be recovered.

Helpful tips

When searching, try to use a unique fioeld, such as an invoice number. In the example above, there might be many entries for Adams & Sons, but a cheque number, or invoice number should be unique.

If you find you have wrongly "corrected" an entry, **[Clk]** on [Restore]. Some transactions are better voided. **[Clk]** on [Void Transaction] in the [Edit] menu, then on [Record]. Quicken inserts "Void" before the payee's name and marks the transaction Cleared as well as removing the amount. Voiding is particularly appropriate if you need to cancel a cheque, as you will still have a complete record of the cheque numbers.

Errors & Adjustments

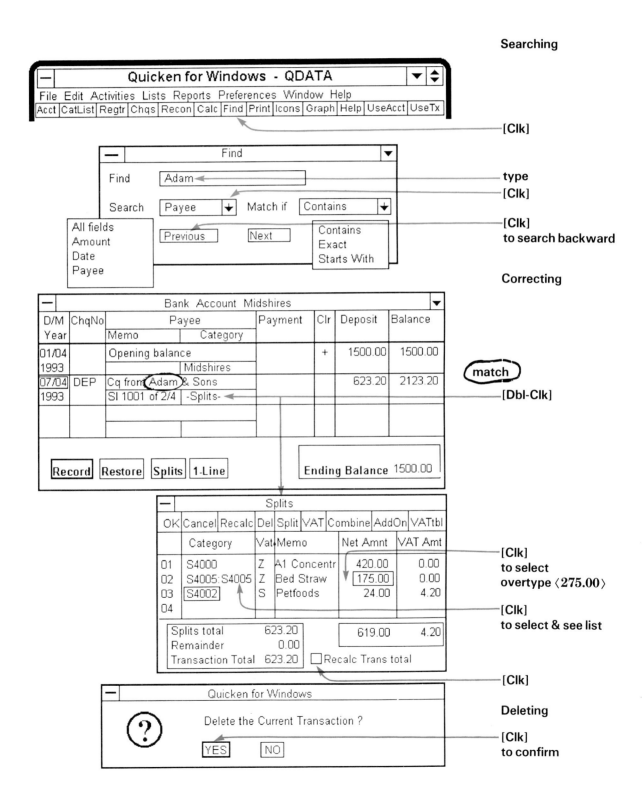

Quicken for Windows - QDATA

File Edit Activities Lists Reports Preferences Window Help
Acct | CatList | Regtr | Chqs | Recon | Calc | Find | Print | Icons | Graph | Help | UseAcct | UseTx

[Clk]

Find

Find	Adam		type
			[Clk]
Search	Payee	Match if	Contains	[Clk]
			to search backward

All fields
Amount
Date
Payee

Previous   Next

Contains
Exact
Starts With

Correcting

Bank Account Midshires

D/M Year	ChqNo	Payee / Memo Category	Payment	Clr	Deposit	Balance
01/04 1993		Opening balance / Midshires		+	1500.00	1500.00
07/04 1993	DEP	Cq from Adam & Sons / SI 1001 of 2/4 -Splits-			623.20	2123.20

match

[Dbl-Clk]

Record Restore Splits 1-Line   Ending Balance 1500.00

Splits

OK | Cancel | Recalc | Del | Split | VAT | Combine | AddOn | VATtbl

	Category	Vat	Memo	Net Amnt	VAT Amt
01	S4000	Z	A1 Concentr	420.00	0.00
02	S4005:S4005	Z	Bed Straw	175.00	0.00
03	S4002	S	Petfoods	24.00	4.20
04					

Splits total	623.20
Remainder	0.00
Transaction Total	623.20

619.00   4.20

☐ Recalc Trans total

[Clk]
to select
overtype ⟨275.00⟩

[Clk]
to select & see list

[Clk]

Quicken for Windows

(?) Delete the Current Transaction ?

YES   NO

Deleting

[Clk]
to confirm

15

Petty Cash

Most businesses use a petty cash account to record minor purchases; in Quicken, cash transactions can be recorded in the current account transaction register, and home users may prefer simply to do this, allocating the sums to a separate category such as "Cash Payments". However, a separate Petty Cash account provides better control, and should be the choice of business users.

Instructions

- Set up a new account – [Petty Cash]. **[Clk]** on [Accts] in the icon bar, and when the [Account List] appears, **[Clk]** on the [New] button. **[Clk]** on [Cash Account], then [OK] in the [Select Account Type] window.
- Type the account name ⟨**Petty Cash**⟩ and the balance ⟨**0.00**⟩ in the [New Account Information] window and **[Clk]** on [OK].
- Return to the [Midshires] transaction register, and enter the withdrawal of £100.00 from a cash dispenser to provide the cash float. This is a transfer from the source (current) account to the destination (petty cash) account, achieved by inserting [Petty Cash] as the category. **[Clk]** on [OK] to record the transaction.
- Open the [Account List], **[Clk]** on [Petty Cash] to select it, then on the [Use] button. The [Petty Cash] transaction register will open: – it should resemble the first illustration.
- Regularly, and at least once a week, adjust the cash balance to reflect the cash in hand, and account for the difference.
- **[Clk]** on [Activities] to open the menu, and select [Update Balances]. **[Clk]** on [Update Cash Balance] to open the [Update Account Balance] window.
- Count the petty cash on hand, and type this figure ⟨**84.46**⟩ in the [Update this account balance to] field. You should have receipts or some other evidence of payment to cover this. Leave the [Category] field blank unless only one category is involved. **[Clk]** on [OK].
- **[Clk]** on [Splits] to apportion the balance adjustment as follows:
  01 Office – Z – Staff tea & coffee – 10.54
  02 Repairs – N – J Brown window blind – 5.00
  [Clk] on [OK] to close the [Splits] window, and on [Record] to finish.

Helpful tips

Note the VAT code "N" applied to businesses not registered for VAT.

Cash from counter sales should not pass through [Petty Cash], but should be banked without delay and posted straight to the current account transaction register.

It is prudent to keep a petty cash float rather than dip into the till as the need arises. Although the disbursements may be relatively small, they should be supported by receipts, and recorded in the first instance in a Petty Cash Book.

Petty Cash

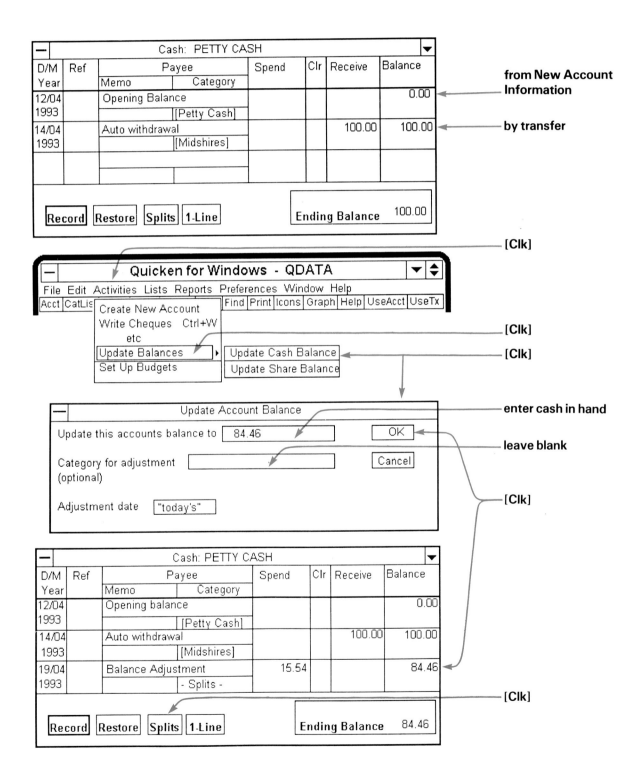

		Cash: PETTY CASH				
D/M Year	Ref	Payee	Spend	Clr	Receive	Balance
		Memo	Category			
12/04 1993		Opening Balance				0.00
			[Petty Cash]			
14/04 1993		Auto withdrawal			100.00	100.00
			[Midshires]			

Record **Restore** **Splits** **1-Line**   Ending Balance   100.00

from New Account Information ←

by transfer ←

[Clk]

Quicken for Windows - QDATA

File Edit Activities Lists Reports Preferences Window Help

Acct | CatLis | | | Find | Print | Icons | Graph | Help | UseAcct | UseTx

Create New Account
Write Cheques   Ctrl+W
etc
Update Balances   ▸   Update Cash Balance
Set Up Budgets   Update Share Balance

[Clk]
[Clk]

Update Account Balance

Update this accounts balance to   84.46   OK

Category for adjustment
(optional)   Cancel

Adjustment date   "today's"

enter cash in hand →

leave blank →

[Clk]

		Cash: PETTY CASH				
D/M Year	Ref	Payee	Spend	Clr	Receive	Balance
		Memo	Category			
12/04 1993		Opening balance				0.00
			[Petty Cash]			
14/04 1993		Auto withdrawal			100.00	100.00
			[Midshires]			
19/04 1993		Balance Adjustment	15.54			84.46
			- Splits -			

Record **Restore** **Splits** **1-Line**   Ending Balance   84.46

[Clk]

[Clk]

17

Standing Orders

Details of payments by standing order or direct debit which you have arranged through your bank should be entered in Quicken. The payments will be recorded in the transaction register on the date specified.

Instructions

● **[Clk]** on [Lists] to open the menu and from it select [Standing Orders].

● The [Standing Order List] will have no entries; **[Clk]** on the [New] button to open the [Set Up Standing Order] window.

● Press **[Tab]** to accept the default entries and to move on after typing the information in the [Payee], [Amount], [Next Payment Due] and [Memo] fields.

● **[Clk]** on [OK] when you have finished. The [Splits] window will open if you have entered a category with a VAT code: check that this is correct, then **[Clk]** [OK] to close the [Splits] window.

● Home users who wish to divide a payment between categories should **[Clk]** on the [Splits] button.

● **[Clk]** [OK] again when you have returned to the [Set Up] window. A message will confirm that the direct debit or standing order has been set up. The [Standing Order List] will reappear.

● Set up the other regular payments shown in the list at the foot of the illustration page.

Helpful tips

If you make more than one payment to the same payee, the name in the [Payee] field must be varied: "Jardine" would so, or "Messrs Jardine".

The standing order routine may be used if you receive a regular payment into your bank account; in the [Type] field, select [Dep]. Use this method if your salary is paid directly into your bank account; the [Splits] window will accommodate deductions for PAYE. pension contributions and other details.

If the [Amount] field is left blank, or contains an estimate, you will need to enter the amount shown in your bank statement in the transaction register.

You may ensure that regular payments by cheque are not overlooked by entering details in the [Set Up Standing Order] window, replacing [StdOrd] in the [Number] field with an asterisk. This will cause Quicken to create a cheque which you can edit at the [Write Cheques] window and print.

To print a list of your standing orders and direct debits, simply **[Clk]** on [Print] in the icon bar with the [Standing Order List] on screen.

The [Number] field in the [Set Up Standing Order] window is so called because the information – [StdOrd], for example – is posted to the [ChqNo] field in the transaction register.

Standing Orders

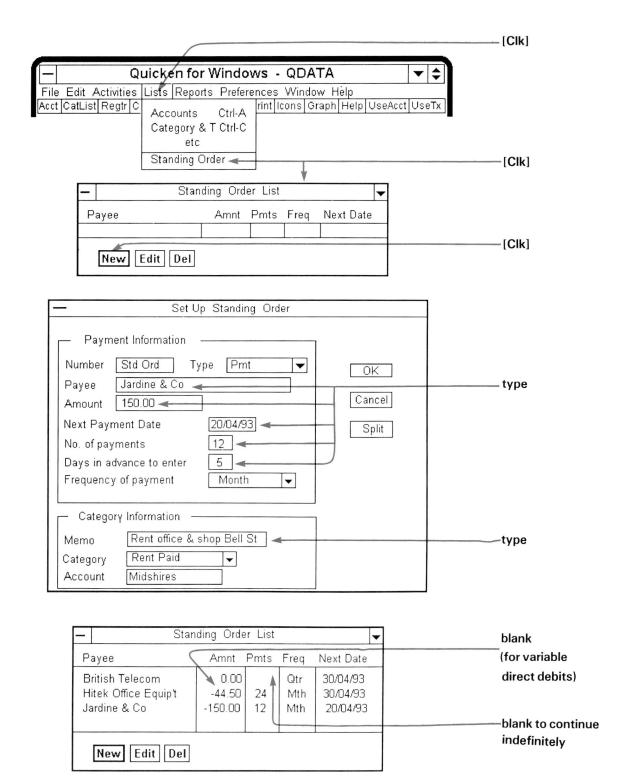

[Clk]

[Clk]

[Clk]

type

type

blank
(for variable
direct debits)

blank to continue
indefinitely

19

Credit Cards

Home users who pay off credit card bills in full do not need to make use of Quicken's credit card accounts. They should simply record the payment in the current account transaction register – either manually from their cheque book counterfoil, or automatically from the [Write Cheques] window with "Intuit" cheques – and make use of [Splits] if the payment covers more than one category. Business users will prefer to have a record of each transaction, and to be able at any time to find out the balance outstanding. These aims are best achieved by setting up credit card accounts – a separate account for each card that you use.

Instructions

- Set up a new account – [Midshire Visa] – using the procedure described when setting up the Petty Cash account. The details for the [New Account Information] window are in the first illustration on the facing page.
- As you use your credit card, enter details from the transaction slips in the transaction register. Open the [Accounts List], highlight [Visa] and **[Clk]** the [Use] button. The illustration contains some examples.
- Each month, at a date which will be determined by your statement date, you should reconcile the items recorded in the register with the statement before making a payment.
- Open the credit card register, **[Clk]** on [Recon] in the icon bar. Complete the [Credit Card Statement Information] window, remembering to add any interest charges in the [Financial Charges] box.
- **[Clk]** [OK] and the [Pay Credit Card Bill] window will open. **[Clk]** each transaction which appears on your credit card statement to mark it cleared.
- If the statement contains items that are missing from your accounts, **[Clk]** [Go to] and enter them in the register.
- When the [Difference] field is zero, **[Clk]** [Done]. The [Make Credit Card Payment] window will open. Depending on whether you are using "Intuit" printed, or handwritten cheques, Quicken will transfer you to either the [Write Cheques] screen or the current account transaction register, where you can complete the transaction.

Helpful tips

Quicken will memorise the information and use it when you next make a payment on this credit card account.

Credit card statements are usually received well in advance of the date of settlement, and writing a Quicken post-dated cheque will ensure that payment is not overlooked.

Using a credit card for minor purchases has some advantages over cash – you have an independent record of the transaction, there is no need for an antry in the Petty Cash Book, taking out cash in reimbursement, or scribbling IOUs for change owed by or owing to petty cash.

Credit Cards

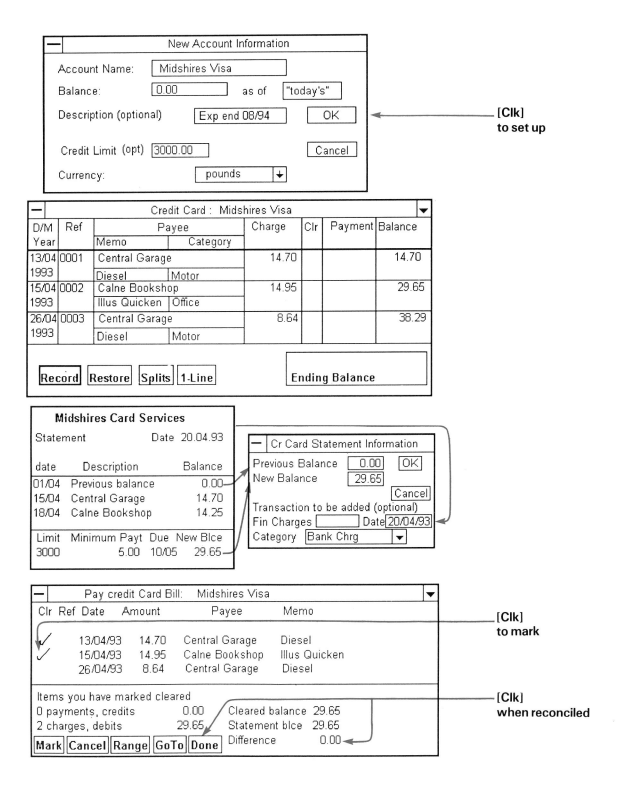

New Account Information

Account Name: Midshires Visa
Balance: 0.00 as of "today's"
Description (optional) Exp end 08/94 OK
Credit Limit (opt) 3000.00 Cancel
Currency: pounds

[Clk]
to set up

Credit Card : Midshires Visa

D/M Year	Ref	Payee		Charge	Clr	Payment	Balance
		Memo	Category				
13/04 1993	0001	Central Garage		14.70			14.70
		Diesel	Motor				
15/04 1993	0002	Calne Bookshop		14.95			29.65
		Illus Quicken	Office				
26/04 1993	0003	Central Garage		8.64			38.29
		Diesel	Motor				

Record Restore Splits 1-Line   Ending Balance

Midshires Card Services

Statement   Date 20.04.93

date	Description	Balance
01/04	Previous balance	0.00
15/04	Central Garage	14.70
18/04	Calne Bookshop	14.25

Limit	Minimum Payt	Due	New Blce
3000	5.00	10/05	29.65

Cr Card Statement Information

Previous Balance 0.00 OK
New Balance 29.65
Cancel
Transaction to be added (optional)
Fin Charges [ ] Date 20/04/93
Category Bank Chrg

Pay credit Card Bill: Midshires Visa

Clr	Ref	Date	Amount	Payee	Memo
✓		13/04/93	14.70	Central Garage	Diesel
✓		15/04/93	14.95	Calne Bookshop	Illus Quicken
		26/04/93	8.64	Central Garage	Diesel

Items you have marked cleared
0 payments, credits   0.00   Cleared balance 29.65
2 charges, debits   29.65   Statement blce   29.65

Mark Cancel Range GoTo Done   Difference   0.00

[Clk]
to mark

[Clk]
when reconciled

21

Printing Cheques

Credit purchases were dealt with by writing post-dated cheques, the aim being to enter the liability in your accounts as soon as the invoice arrives, and to time payments so that you neither incur penalties for late settlement, nor needlessly strain your cash flow.

Instructions

- Load the cheques into your printer, and make sure that it is on line.
- See that the printer to be used for printing cheques is selected. Open the [File] menu, select [Printer Set Up] and then [Cheque Printer Set Up..]. You will probably find that Quicken and the Windows Print Manager have already done this. **[Clk]** [OK].
- **[Clk]** [Cheque] in the icon bar to open the [Write Cheques] window: the balances at the foot of the window include [Cheques To Print].
- **[Clk]** [Print] in the icon bar, and the [Print Cheques: Midshires] window will open.
- **[Clk]** the [Sample] button, read the warning message, and **[Clk]** [OK].
- Taking care not to move it, examine the sample cheque: if it has printed correctly **[Clk]** [OK]. If not, correct horizontal misalignment by hand, and vertical misalignment by typing in the [Position Number] box the number that the "Pointer Line" on the sample cheque is pointing to.
- **[Clk]** [OK]. Quicken will adjust the cheques in the printer and print another sample. This should be correctly aligned. Make a note of the position number in line with the print head, and use this when you next load cheques for printing.
- Return to the [Print Cheques] window. Type the number of the first cheque in the [First Cheque Number] box.
- **[Clk]** the [Selected Cheques] button, then [Choose..]. By this means you can review the cheques that are about to be printed.
- The final column of the [Select Cheques to Print] window shows "Print" against cheques that are due for printing in accordance with the Billminder setting – the default is 3 days in advance.
- To mark a cheque for printing, **[Dbl-Clk]** it: if you do not wish to print one of the selected cheques, **[Dbl-Clk]** will cancel the mark.
- **[Clk]** [OK] to close the window then **[Clk]** [Print] in the [Print Cheques] window.
- When printing is finished you will be asked to confirm that the cheques printed correctly.

Helpful tip

To change the setting in Billminder, open the [Preferences] menu, select [Billminder] and type a new number in the box.

Printing Cheques

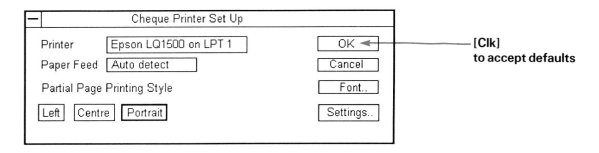

Cheque Printer Set Up	
Printer	Epson LQ1500 on LPT 1	OK ◄——— [Clk] to accept defaults

Printer Epson LQ1500 on LPT 1   OK ◄
Paper Feed Auto detect   Cancel
Partial Page Printing Style   Font..
[Left] [Centre] [Portrait]   Settings..

— **[Clk] to accept defaults**

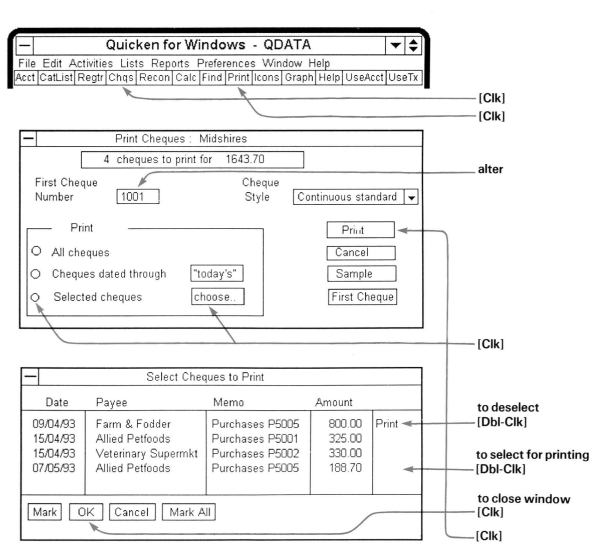

Quicken for Windows - QDATA

File Edit Activities Lists Reports Preferences Window Help
Acct | CatList | Regtr | Chqs | Recon | Calc | Find | Print | Icons | Graph | Help | UseAcct | UseTx

— **[Clk]**
— **[Clk]**

Print Cheques : Midshires

4 cheques to print for   1643.70

— **alter**

First Cheque
Number   1001   Cheque Style   Continuous standard ▼

Print
○ All cheques   Print ◄
○ Cheques dated through   "today's"   Cancel
○ Selected cheques   choose..   Sample
                                          First Cheque

— **[Clk]**

Select Cheques to Print

Date	Payee	Memo	Amount	
09/04/93	Farm & Fodder	Purchases P5005	800.00	Print
15/04/93	Allied Petfoods	Purchases P5001	325.00	
15/04/93	Veterinary Supermkt	Purchases P5002	330.00	
07/05/93	Allied Petfoods	Purchases P5005	188.70	

[Mark] [OK] [Cancel] [Mark All]

to deselect
[Dbl-Clk]

to select for printing
[Dbl-Clk]

to close window
[Clk]

[Clk]

23

Reports

From time to time you may wish to review some aspect of your business or personal finances. Quicken provides a good range of standard reports which will meet most requirements, and you can also define your own reports by selecting options and filters to modify any of the standard reports or the four custom reports – Transaction, Summary, Budget and Account Balances. These are templates on which are based most of Quicken's Business, Home and Investment reports.

Instructions

- To produce a standard report, simply **[Clk]** [Reports] in the menu bar, then select [Business] from the menu and, say, [Cash Flow] from the sub-menu. The [Create Cash Flow Report] window will open: **[Clk]** [OK] to see the report with default settings.

- To modify the standard report, **[Clk]** [Settings..] and, in Cash Flow, the [Create Summary Report] window will open, giving the opportunity to choose options and specify filters. Experiment with these to find what suits you.

- To create a custom report in the form of an Audit Trail for your accountant, open the [Reports] menu and select [Custom]. **[Clk]** on [Transaction..]. This report, in default form, lists individual transactions in the bank current account.

- The Audit Trail should include transactions on all accounts. When the [Create Transaction Report] screen opens, study the default entries.

- Give your report a name ⟨ **Audit Trail** ⟩, and set the dates you require – the drop-down lists include "text" dates like that shown in the example, which are calculated from today's date, and are not actual dates independent of today's date.

- It is helpful to subtotal by account, so select [Account] from the drop-down list.

- The important alteration is to **[Clk]** the [All Accounts] button to change the [Accounts to Report on] from [Current (Midshires)].

- **[Clk]** [Options] and change the [Memo/Category Display] to [Category only]. **[Clk]** [OK] and when the [Create Report] screen returns, **[Clk]** [Filters]. There are no restrictions by default, and if you have doubts, **[Clk]** on [Reset] to return to the default settings.

- **[Clk]** [OK] to close the [Filters] window; when you return to the [Create Report] window, **[Clk]** [OK] to see your report on screen.

- To memorise the settings for future use, **[Clk]** on [Memorise] in the button bar at the top of the report window.

- **[Clk]** [Close] when you have finished with the report on screen.

- To recall a memorised report, open the [Reports] menu and choose [Memorised..]; select the report you require from the list.

Reports

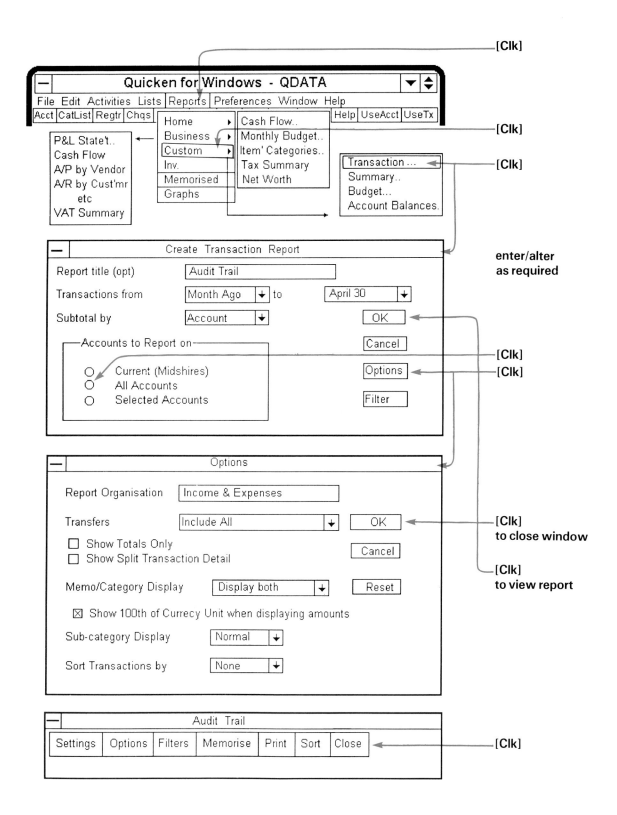

[Clk]

Quicken for Windows - QDATA

File Edit Activities Lists Reports Preferences Window Help

Acct CatList Regtr Chqs | Help UseAcct UseTx

Home ▶ | Cash Flow..
Business ▶ | Monthly Budget..
Custom ▶ | Item' Categories..
Inv. | Tax Summary
Memorised | Net Worth
Graphs

P&L State't..
Cash Flow
A/P by Vendor
A/R by Cust'mr
etc
VAT Summary

[Clk]

Transaction ...
Summary..
Budget...
Account Balances.

[Clk]

enter/alter
as required

Create Transaction Report

Report title (opt)   Audit Trail

Transactions from   Month Ago ▼ to   April 30 ▼

Subtotal by   Account ▼   OK

┌─Accounts to Report on─────────┐   Cancel
│ ○   Current (Midshires)   │   Options
│ ○   All Accounts   │
│ ○   Selected Accounts   │   Filter
└───────────────────────────────┘

[Clk]
[Clk]

Options

Report Organisation   Income & Expenses

Transfers   Include All   ▼   OK

☐ Show Totals Only   Cancel
☐ Show Split Transaction Detail

Memo/Category Display   Display both   ▼   Reset

☒ Show 100th of Currecy Unit when displaying amounts

Sub-category Display   Normal   ▼

Sort Transactions by   None   ▼

[Clk]
to close window

[Clk]
to view report

Audit Trail

Settings | Options | Filters | Memorise | Print | Sort | Close

[Clk]

Bank Reconciliation

The closing balance of your bank statement should be reconciled monthly with Quicken's current account transaction register to ensure the accuracy of the entries in both. The process is similar to that used when reconciling a credit card statement.

Instructions

- If the transaction register of the account you wish to reconcile is not active, **[Clk]** [Accts] on the icon bar, select the account from the [Accounts List] and **[Clk]** [Use].

- **[Clk]** [Recon] on the icon bar to open the [Reconcile Register with Bank Statement] window. After the first reconciliation, if you did not print out, or cannot find, the previous report, **[Clk]** the [Report] button to reprint the last reconciliation report. A reconciliation report is only stored until the next reconciliation.

- Compare the opening balance with that on your statement, then type the closing balance from the bank statement in the [Bank Statement Ending Balance] box.

- Enter any bank charges or interest earned; the default date is "today's", but you may prefer to alter this to the statement date for the item.

- Enter a category – Quicken will automatically insert it in the category box at future reconciliations – and **[Clk]** [OK] to continue.

- The [Reconcile Bank Account – Midshires] window will open, displaying a list of uncleared transactions from the current account register.

- Mark "cleared" all transactions in the [Reconcile Bank Account] window that match entries in your bank statement. To mark an entry "cleared", simply **[Clk]** it, or select it by moving the selection highlight and then **[Clk]** [Mark] or press **[Spacebar]**. If you incorrectly mark a transaction, **[Clk]** the item again to unmark it.

- Don't forget to tick items on your bank statement as you mark them in the register.

- Select the appropriate entry and **[Clk]** [Go To] to return to the transaction register and make corrections. To enter a missing transaction, make sure the selection highlight is on a blank line in the [Reconcile Bank Account] window before you **[Clk]** [Go To].

- When the [Difference] at the foot of the [Reconcile] window is zero, **[Clk]** [Done] and create the reconciliation report at the [Reconciliation Report Set Up] window. On most occasions a [Summary and Uncleared] report will suffice.

Helpful tip

You will need your bank paying in book to reconcile deposits shown on the statement as a single total with the individual items in the register.

Bank Reconciliation

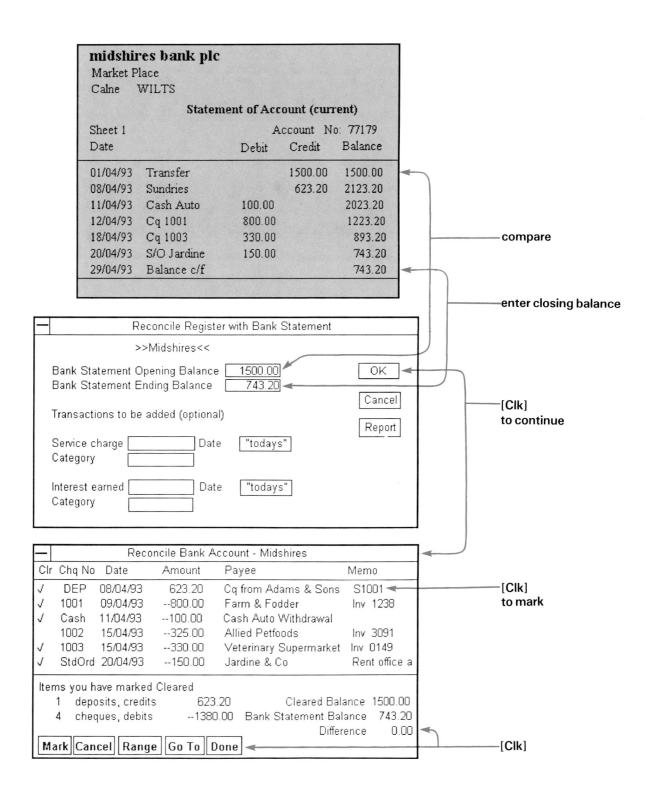

midshires bank plc				
Market Place				
Calne WILTS				
Statement of Account (current)				
Sheet 1		Account No: 77179		
Date		Debit	Credit	Balance
01/04/93	Transfer		1500.00	1500.00
08/04/93	Sundries		623.20	2123.20
11/04/93	Cash Auto	100.00		2023.20
12/04/93	Cq 1001	800.00		1223.20
18/04/93	Cq 1003	330.00		893.20
20/04/93	S/O Jardine	150.00		743.20
29/04/93	Balance c/f			743.20

— compare

— enter closing balance

Reconcile Register with Bank Statement

>>Midshires<<

Bank Statement Opening Balance [1500.00]   [OK]

Bank Statement Ending Balance [743.20]

[Cancel]

Transactions to be added (optional)

[Report]

Service charge [   ] Date ["todays"]
Category [   ]

Interest earned [   ] Date ["todays"]
Category [   ]

[Clk]
to continue

Reconcile Bank Account - Midshires

Clr	Chq No	Date	Amount	Payee	Memo
√	DEP	08/04/93	623.20	Cq from Adams & Sons	S1001
√	1001	09/04/93	--800.00	Farm & Fodder	Inv 1238
√	Cash	11/04/93	--100.00	Cash Auto Withdrawal	
	1002	15/04/93	--325.00	Allied Petfoods	Inv 3091
√	1003	15/04/93	--330.00	Veterinary Supermarket	Inv 0149
√	StdOrd	20/04/93	--150.00	Jardine & Co	Rent office a

Items you have marked Cleared
1	deposits, credits	623.20	Cleared Balance	1500.00
4	cheques, debits	--1380.00	Bank Statement Balance	743.20
			Difference	0.00

[Mark] [Cancel] [Range] [Go To] [Done]

[Clk]
to mark

[Clk]

27

Paying Staff

Although this section and some of those following are not directly relevant to home users, they provide practice in working with accounts, categories and transfers. Quicken can help with many payroll tasks – including writing and printing cheques, deductions from pay, the employer's liability for tax and National Insurance, reports for end of year tax forms – although it cannot automatically perform computations of employees' earnings or calculate deductions like PAYE which are based on personal circumstances.

A company payroll has two expenses – gross pay and the employer's National Insurance contribution – for which categories must be created, and a number of liabilities relating mainly to deductions – for which accounts must be set up.

Instructions

- **[Clk]** [Cat List] on the icon bar, then the [New] button, and create tax related subcategories for "Gross Pay" and "Company NI" (which must be distinguished from employees' NI contributions).

- **[Clk]** [Accts] on the icon bar, then the [New] button, and open liability accounts for payroll deductions. Each type of deduction must have a separate account, and the name must begin with "Payroll" to enable Quicken to assemble payroll information. The accounts are [Other Liability] type accounts.

- Turn off VAT tracking for these accounts: move the selection highlight to the account and **[Clk]** [Edit]. When the [Edit Account Information] window opens, **[Clk]** the [Track VAT] check box to remove the check.

- If necessary, create subcategories for company contributions to such items as a company pension scheme or medical care plan, and accounts for the deductions from employees' earnings.

- To write payroll cheques, open the current account that you use to pay salaries and wages, and **[Clk]** [Cheques] in the icon bar. Fill in the date and the employee's name. **[Clk]** [Splits] and when the window opens put [Payroll:Gross Pay] in the first line [Category] window; then enter the amount of the gross pay.

- On lines 2 and 3 enter the deduction liability accounts in the [Category] window, and the amount of each deduction as a negative sum. Leave the next few lines blank except for a hyphen in the [Memo] field to prevent Quicken from closing up the blank line.

- On line 9 if VAT tracking is ON; on line 17 if VAT tracking is OFF, enter the positive amount of the company NI contribution in the category [Payroll:Company NI]. On line 10 (or line 18) enter the compensating negative amount of the company NI contribution to the liability account [Payroll NI] – as indicated in the illustration. **[Clk]** [OK] then [Record].

Helpful tip

The compensating amounts do not affect the employee's cheque, but they do record your tax liability. By entering these details below line 8 (VAT ON) or 16 (VAT OFF), they will not be shown on the printed voucher cheque.

Paying Staff

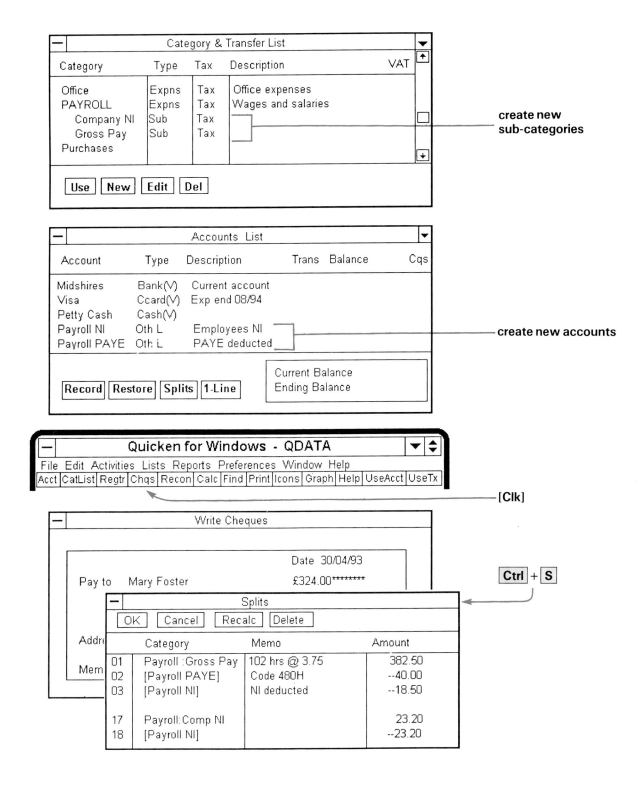

create new
sub-categories

create new accounts

[Clk]

Ctrl + S

29

Payroll Tasks

After paying staff the major payroll tasks which arise involve making payments to the Inland Revenue of PAYE deducted and NI contributions from both employee and company. Payments to other organisations, such as the insurance company running your pension scheme may also be necessary. At the end of the year you will also need to complete a payroll tax form.

Instructions

- Payments to the Inland Revenue are made from your current account, using the [Splits] window to combine PAYE and NI in one cheque.
- Press [Ctrl+A] to open the [Accounts List]. The figure in the balance column of the two Payroll accounts shows your liability to the Collector of Taxes.
- Select the [Midshires] current account, and press [Ctrl+W] to open the [Write Cheques] window. Fill in the payee's name and address, open the [Splits] window and insert the accounts [Payroll-PAYE] amd [Payroll-NI] in the [Category] boxes on lines 01 and 02. [Clk] [OK] to close the [Splits] window and press [Ctrl+M] to memorise the cheque.
- Return to the [Splits] window and fill in the [Memo] and [Amount] fields: the total will be transferred automatically to the cheque when you [Clk] [OK] and written in words when you press [Tab].
- Give a reference in the [Memo] field on the face of the cheque, and when you are finished [Clk] [Record] – or press [Enter] – to record the transaction.
- If you look again at the [Accounts List] you will see that the balance on the PAYE and NI liability accounts has been reduced by the amounts making up the cheque: in the example, reduced to nil.
- Most of the information you need to complete the payroll tax form can be obtained by running the Quicken payroll report. [Clk] on [Reports] in the menu bar, select [Business], then [Payroll]. The report will select only transactions and transfers which begin with the word "Payroll".

Helpful tips

Quicken's ability to memorise transactions is invaluable where payroll is involved. If an employee's pay and deductions do not vary, memorise the completed cheque. If pay varies from month to month, use the template method (described above) and memorise the cheque before you enter figures – or any information which changes.

If you are not using Quicken to print cheques, but still wish to have some of the advantages of writing post-dated cheques, enter your payments in the transaction register under the due date and select [Print] in the [ChqNo] field. When you make out your handwritten cheque return to the register and type the cheque number over "Print" in the [ChqNo] field.

You may prefer to use the [Write Cheques] window to write post-dated cheques, print them in due course (when prompted by "Billminder") on standard paper and copy the details to handwritten cheques.

Payroll Tasks

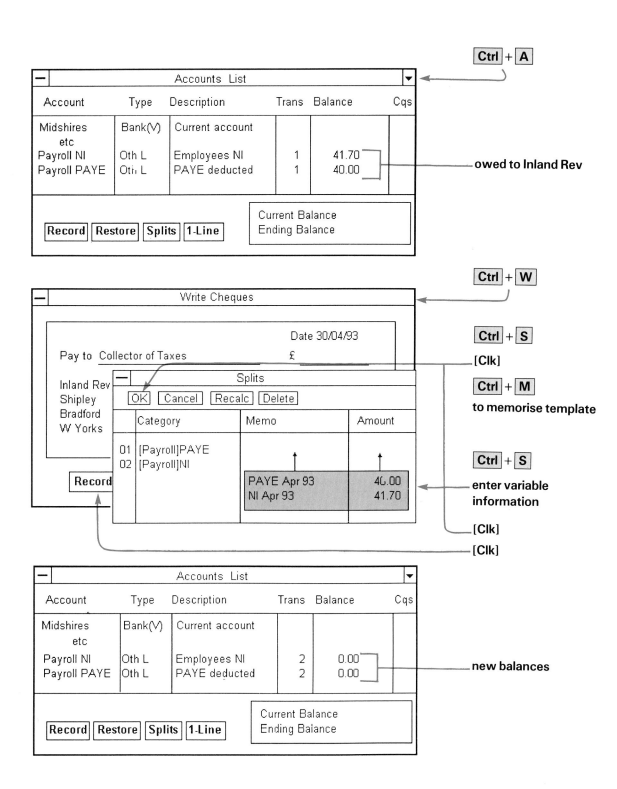

31

The VAT Return

The need to account for VAT seems to consume much time and cause considerable unease. Fortunately, VAT returns are efficiently handled by Quicken, and your burden will be lightened if you have prepared the way correctly. If you are not registered for VAT, you should turn off VAT tracking before you begin.

Instructions

- To complete your VAT return, you need to run the VAT Summary Report. At the menu bar, open the [Reports] menu, select [Business], then from the sub menu choose [VAT Summary].
- In the [VAT Summary Report] window, enter a report title and the date range covering the VAT period for which you want the report. You should specify subtotalling by month. There should be no need to alter the default options and filters. **[Clk]** [OK] to produce the report.
- At the foot of the Summary Report are the figures you need for the VAT 100 Return.
- If you owe tax, issue a cheque in the usual way, using [VAT Control] in the [Category] field: if you reclaim tax, enter the deposit in the current account transaction register – categorise under [VAT Control].
- The VAT Detail Report is an expanded version of the summary report and it is recommended that you should run this report monthly.

Helpful tips

Turn off VAT tracking from the [Preferences] menu; choose [International] and **[Clk]** the [Use VAT] check box to remove the check.

If the standard rate is altered, open the [Activities] menu, select [VAT Table] and make the necessary changes in the [Edit VAT Rates] window.

Categories in the standard [Category & Transfer List] have VAT codes assigned, and for most of the time these will be correct. When you create a new category or sub-category, remember to indicate whether it is tax related, and, if the tax concerned is VAT, assign a code.

If you need to alter any entries involving VAT at the [Splits] screen, remember that Quicken WILL recalculate VAT

if you change the code or the net amount;
but Quicken WILL NOT adjust the net amount

if you alter the figures in the [VAT Amount] field. You must [Recalculate Transaction Total] if you wish to do this.

If your business runs on straightforward cash accounting, recording transactions only when money is paid or received, make sure that VAT tracking is turned on for your current account – or accounts. Turn VAT tracking on or off for individual accounts at the [Edit Account Information] window. Press **[Ctrl+A]** for the [Accounts List]: a V after the account type indicates that VAT tracking is on. Move the selection bar to the account you want and **[Clk]** the [Edit] button. **[Clk]** the [Track VAT] check box.

The VAT Return

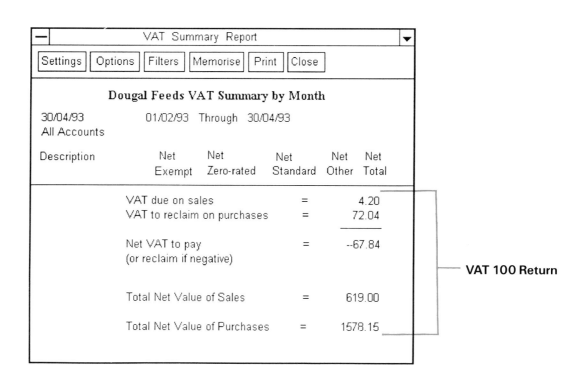

Credit Sales

Many businesses which are predominantly cash trading have some customers who are allowed to purchase goods on credit and settle accounts monthly. In order to control these accounts, it is necessary to make an entry in your books when an invoice is issued. As no money is involved at this stage, you should set up a new account to hold details of the expected income.

Instructions

● Create an [Other Asset] account as indicated in the illustration on the facing page.
● Select the account, **[Clk]** [Edit] and clear the [Track VAT] check box to turn off VAT tracking for this account.
● Prepare invoices for entry by summarising them in a book or on a sheet, including details of categories if an invoice contains more than one.
● Enter the invoices in the [Credit Sales] account; if the invoice number is too long, use the [Memo] field instead of the [ChqNo] field. In the [Memo] field you may also enter the date due.

Helpful tips

"Quickfill" will memorise your transaction automatically, and your customers' names will appear on the drop-down list in the [Payee] field; this makes for speedy and accurate entry.

If you issue a credit note to a customer, record it in a similar way, entering the amount in the [Decrease] field.

Note that a credit sales account is an example of accrual – as opposed to cash – accounting. You may use Quicken for a complete accrual accounting system and this has important consequences for VAT. The "tax point" at which you become liable for VAT, and must, therefore, record VAT in your accounts, moves from the date payment occurs, to the date an invoice is issued or received.

VAT must not now appear in your current account transaction register, which should have VAT tracking switched OFF, but in the asset and liability accounts – the Sales and Purchases ledgers – which need VAT tracking ON, unless you have agreed the VAT cash accounting scheme with your local VAT office.

Credit Sales

```
┌─────────────────────────────────────────────────────┐
│ ─            New Account Information                  │
│                                                       │
│  Account Name:    ┌─────────────────┐   ┌────────┐    │
│                   │ Credit Sales    │   │  OK    │    │
│  Balance:         ┌─────────────────┐   ┌────────┐    │
│                   │     0.00        │   │ Cancel │    │
│  Description (optional)  ┌──────────────────┐         │
│                         │ Accounts Receivable│        │
│  Currency:              ┌─────────────┬───┐           │
│                         │   pounds    │ ↓ │           │
│                         └─────────────┴───┘           │
└─────────────────────────────────────────────────────┘
```

Dougal Feeds of Calne		Invoice Summary Sheet		
Inv no	Category Description	Net Amount	VAT	Date
S1001	Adam & Sons (Farmers) Ltd			10/04/93
	4000 A1 Conc/Pigibran	420.00	Z	
	4001 Dogomeat/Kitibrek	24.00	S	
	4005 Bedding Straw	175.00	Z	
S1002	Manfred Stutz (Circus)			10/04/93
	4000 Racehorse nuts	1250.00	Z	
	4005 Comfistable shavings	750.00	Z	
S1003	J R Norris (Petcare)			11/04/93
	4001 Dogibix/Kitibrek	120.00	S	
	4002 Veterinary drugs	35.00	Z	
	4005 Pet accessories	155.00	S	
S1004	Khalil Stables (Lambourn)			11/04/93
	4005 NZ Horse blankets	238.50	S	
S1005	Alan Afghans			12/04/93
	4001 Houndmix	144.66	S	
	4002 Xworm/Canivax	72.00	Z	
	4005 Comfikennel bedding	150.00	S	

D/M Year	ChqNo	Payee / Memo Category	Decrease	Clr	Increase	Balance
		Other Asset Credit Sales				▼
01/04 1993		Opening Balance [Credit Sales]		+		0.00
10/04	S1001	Adams & Sons (				

Record Restore Splits

```
┌──────────────────────────────────────────────────┐
│ ─                   Splits                         │
│   ┌────┐ ┌──────┐ ┌───────┐ ┌────────┐             │
│   │ OK │ │Cancel│ │ Recalc│ │ Delete │             │
│                                                    │
│      Category        Memo          Amount          │
│  01  Sales:S4000   A! Conc/Pigibran    420.00      │
│  02  Sales:S4001   Dogomeat/Kitibrek    24.00      │
│  03  Sales:S4005:S40 Bedding straw     175.00      │
│  04                                                │
└──────────────────────────────────────────────────┘
```

35

Receiving Payment

Having made some sales on credit, and recorded the invoices as accounts receivable, the next step is to deal with incoming cheques: these may be in full or part settlement of an invoice. The procedure below assumes that you use cash accounting.

Instructions

- As you receive cheques, prepare them for posting: enter details on a form like that illustrated, or in a day book. The batch total should agree with the total on a bank paying-in slip.
- Post the cheques received to your current account transaction register, using the [Splits] window [Category] field to transfer the net amounts to the [Credit Sales] asset account, and to enter both net and VAT amounts.
- Quicken automatically transfers the VAT amount to the [VAT Control] account.
- Open the [Credit Sales] account and mark with an asterisk in the [Clr] field both the invoice and the corresponding payment. **[Clk]** [Record] after clearing each transaction.
- Record the other cheques received in the current account transaction register. Part payments are treated similarly to full payments, but do not mark the transaction as cleared.

Helpful tips

If you follow accrual accounting, you will enter the payment in the [Credit Sales] transaction register: use the drop-down list to enter the customer's name in the [Payee] field, enter the amount in the [Decrease] field, put an asterisk in the [Clr] field, quote the invoice number in the [Memo] field, and the name of the current account in the [Category] field. **[Clk]** [Record].

Find the invoice entry in the [Credit Sales] register, using [Find] to search for the invoice number, mark the invoice cleared and **[Clk]** [Record].

The standard business report "Accounts Receivable by Customer" will list unpaid invoices provided you remember to clear paid invoices and their payments. To run the report, open the [Reports] menu, select the [Business] sub menu and choose [A/R by Customer]. When the [Select Accounts to Include] window opens, include only the [Credit Sales] account.

To adapt this report to show only overdue accounts, **[Clk]** [Settings..] in the [Create A/R by Customer] and set the ending date to "today's" date, less the number of days you allow for settlement. If you take the report on the last day of April, setting the date range from 1st January to 1st April will exclude all invoices dated 2nd April and later.

Knowing the cash position of a business is very important. The first line of defence is the transaction register, where the ending balance takes into account post-dated cheques written at the [Write Cheques] window; there is the standard cash flow report and as well as the accounts receivable reports, provided you enter all bills payable as printable cheques at the transaction register, you can run the [Accounts Payable by Vendor] report.

Receiving Payment

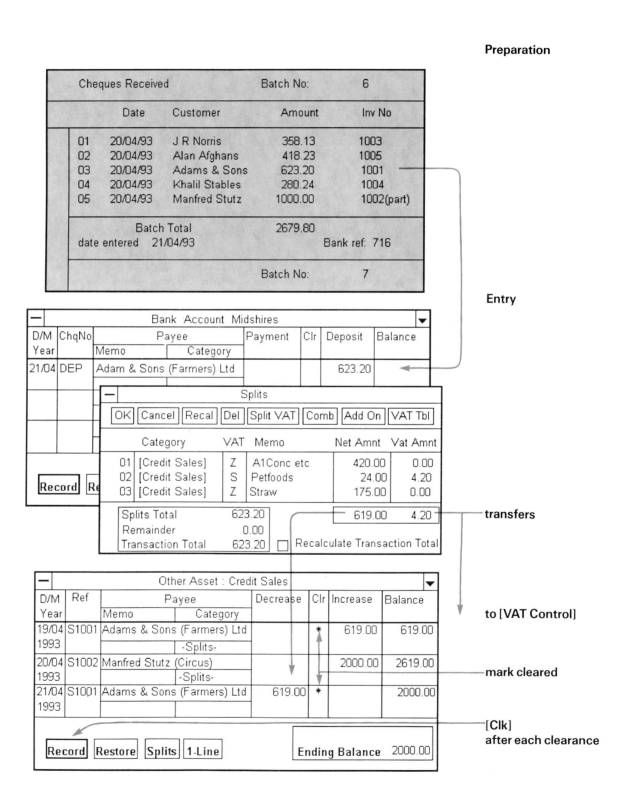

Cheques Received			Batch No:	6
	Date	Customer	Amount	Inv No
01	20/04/93	J R Norris	358.13	1003
02	20/04/93	Alan Afghans	418.23	1005
03	20/04/93	Adams & Sons	623.20	1001
04	20/04/93	Khalil Stables	280.24	1004
05	20/04/93	Manfred Stutz	1000.00	1002(part)
	Batch Total		2679.80	
date entered	21/04/93			Bank ref: 716
			Batch No:	7

Entry

Bank Account Midshires

D/M Year	ChqNo	Payee		Payment	Clr	Deposit	Balance
		Memo	Category				
21/04	DEP	Adam & Sons (Farmers) Ltd				623.20	

Record Re

Splits

OK | Cancel | Recal | Del | Split VAT | Comb | Add On | VAT Tbl

	Category	VAT	Memo	Net Amnt	Vat Amnt
01	[Credit Sales]	Z	A1Conc etc	420.00	0.00
02	[Credit Sales]	S	Petfoods	24.00	4.20
03	[Credit Sales]	Z	Straw	175.00	0.00

Splits Total	623.20		619.00	4.20
Remainder	0.00			
Transaction Total	623.20	☐ Recalculate Transaction Total		

transfers

to [VAT Control]

Other Asset : Credit Sales

D/M Year	Ref	Payee		Decrease	Clr	Increase	Balance
		Memo	Category				
19/04 1993	S1001	Adams & Sons (Farmers) Ltd			*	619.00	619.00
			-Splits-				
20/04 1993	S1002	Manfred Stutz (Circus)				2000.00	2619.00
			-Splits-				
21/04 1993	S1001	Adams & Sons (Farmers) Ltd		619.00	*		2000.00

mark cleared

Record | Restore | Splits | 1-Line

Ending Balance	2000.00

[Clk]
after each clearance

37

End of Period Reports

The Profit & Loss Statement summarises income and expenses by category, its final figure – the Total Income/Expense – being your net loss or profit for the period covered by the report. It is based on the summary report. The Balance Sheet groups the asset and liability accounts to compute the difference between total assets and total liabilities – the equity – and is based on the account balances report.

When the end of period is also the year end, you will need to decide whether you are going to close your accounts to protect data from changes.

Instructions

Profit & Loss Report; Balance Sheet

- Open the [Reports] menu, choose the [Business] sub-menu and **[Clk]** [P & L Statement].
- The statement will probably be required in its standard form so there is no need to do more than fill in at the [Create P & L Statement] window the dates of the period you wish the report to cover. **[Clk]** [OK] to generate the report.
- If you wish to shorten the report by submerging sub-categories and sub-classes in the total for the category or class, **[Clk]** [Settings..] and at the [Create Summary Report] window **[Clk]** [Options].
- Open the [Subcategory display] drop-down menu and **[Clk]** [Suppressed]. **[Clk]** [OK] to return to the [Create Summary Report] window, and **[Clk]** [OK] to create the report.
- To produce a Balance Sheet, open the [Reports] menu, select [Business] and choose [Balance Sheet]. **[Clk]** [OK]; there is no need to alter any settings.

Year End

- Quicken does not require you to close accounts at the year end, but many people prefer to do so. There are two approaches.
- Open the [File] menu and **[Clk]** [Year-End Copy]. At the [Year-End Copy] window, **[Clk]** [OK] to accept the default [Archive]. The [Archive] window should not need alteration: **[Clk]** [OK] to proceed.
- Quicken creates an archive file adding last year's date to the name – QDATA93, for example – and copies to it transactions up to and including 31/12/93. The current file is untouched. At the end of 1994, QDATA94 will include data up to 31/12/94.
- **[Clk]** the [Start New Year] button for the alternative; enter a name for the copy of the current file and **[Clk]** [OK].
- The Start New Year method copies your current file under the name you have given, and deletes all transactions in the current file – except uncleared and share investment transactions – that are not of the current year. Eventually you will have a series of archive files each holding one year's data.

End of Period Reports

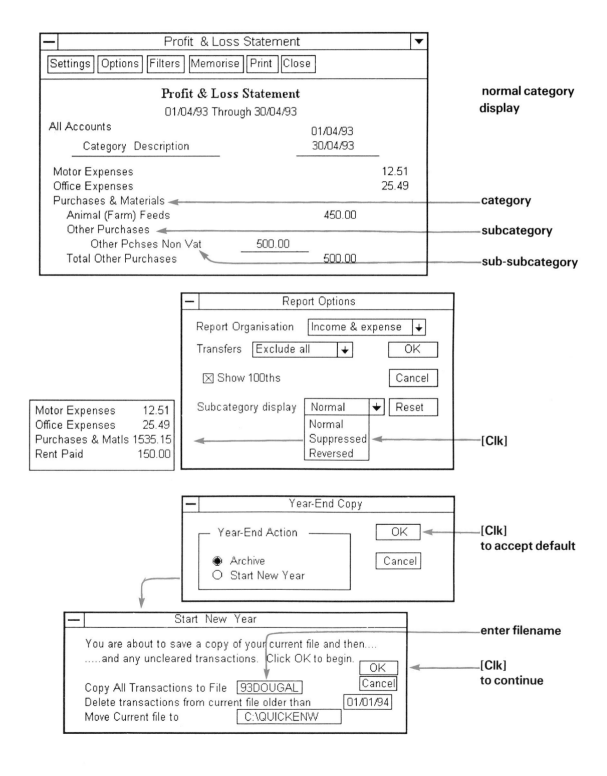

Profit & Loss Statement

Settings | Options | Filters | Memorise | Print | Close

Profit & Loss Statement
01/04/93 Through 30/04/93

All Accounts

01/04/93

Category Description   30/04/93

Motor Expenses   12.51
Office Expenses   25.49
Purchases & Materials ◄──────── category
    Animal (Farm) Feeds   450.00
    Other Purchases ◄──────── subcategory
        Other Pchses Non Vat   500.00
    Total Other Purchases   500.00 ──── sub-subcategory

normal category display

Report Options

Report Organisation | Income & expense | ▼ |

Transfers | Exclude all | ▼ | | OK |

☒ Show 100ths | Cancel |

Subcategory display | Normal | ▼ | | Reset |

Normal
Suppressed ◄──────── [Clk]
Reversed

Motor Expenses   12.51
Office Expenses   25.49
Purchases & Matls 1535.15
Rent Paid   150.00

Year-End Copy

┌─ Year-End Action ─┐ | OK | ◄── [Clk]
                                        to accept default
● Archive | Cancel |
○ Start New Year

Start New Year   ──── enter filename

You are about to save a copy of your current file and then....
.....and any uncleared transactions. Click OK to begin.
                                              | OK | ◄── [Clk]
                                              | Cancel | to continue
Copy All Transactions to File | 93DOUGAL |
Delete transactions from current file older than | 01/01/94 |
Move Current file to | C:\QUICKENW |

Using Classes

While categories are the main method of managing your income and expenditure, Quicken also provides for transactions to be grouped according to class. Classes can be used in many different ways but they are particularly useful for allocating money to sub-accounts, and for bringing together transactions that may be spread over several categories. For example, Dougal Feeds representatives deal in a wide range of products which are categorised according to their nature and to some extent their VAT status; but to calculate the commission due on sales it would be necessary to be able to bring together all sales by each individual representative regardless of category. This can be done with the aid of classes.

Instructions

- To set up a class, open the [Lists] menu and select [Class]. The class list is empty as there is no standard set of classes. **[Clk]** [New].

- Enter the name you wish to give to the class – in the example, a representative's name – and a description if needed.

- **[Clk]** [OK] to set up the class and add it to the class list.

- You may set up classes as you enter transactions: if, after entering a category name you type the forward slash ⟨/⟩, then a class name which is not on the list, you will be asked if you wish to set up a class.

- Once a class is listed, enter it after the category either by opening the [Lists] menu, then choosing [Class] and **[Clk]**ing on the class name you wish to use to paste it in the box, or type the ⟨/⟩ (which Quicken will recognise) and begin typing the name until "Quickfill" completes it for you.

- You may also use subclasses: these are set up as classes. When you are classifying a transaction enter the main class, then type a colon ⟨:⟩ before entering the subclass.

Helpful tips

If you wish to follow the use of classes through to the report stage, set up more classes for representatives, and re-enter the credit sales used in the section on that topic, adding a class after the category.

With the [Credit Sales] register in use, open the [Reports] menu, select [Custom] and then [Transaction]. At the [Filter Report Transactions] window, **[Clk]** the [Select Classes to Include..] checkbox. Include those classes (ie. representatives) whose sales you wish to review and **[Clk]** [OK].

To have in the report only those sales for which you have received payment, **[Clk]** the [Cleared Status: Blank] checkbox to clear it.

You can assign a class to a transaction without giving it a category; this is particularly useful if you use classes as "subaccounts" of your current account so that you can apportion your salary, for example, between a specific fund such as a holiday fund and general expenditure.

Using Classes

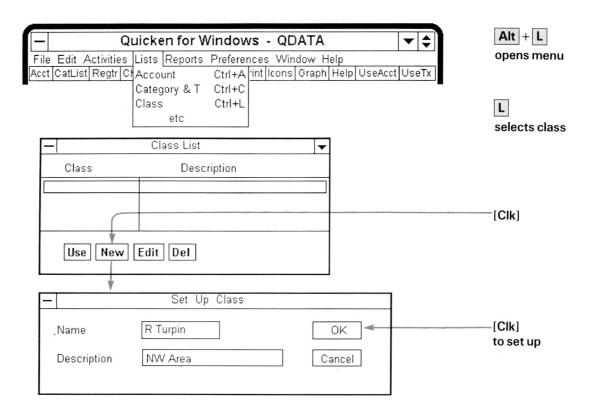

Alt + L
opens menu

L
selects class

[Clk]

[Clk]
to set up

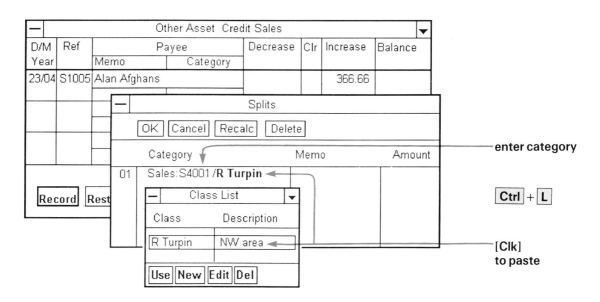

enter category

Ctrl + L

[Clk]
to paste

File Management

The most important task to perform in managing your file involves backing up your data as a precaution against accidental loss. You may also need to set up additional Quicken files or use a password to protect a file.

Instructions

Backing Up & Restoring

- Have some blank, formatted disks ready; place one of the disks in a floppy drive.
- Press **[Alt+F]** to open the [File] menu and **[B]** to choose [Backup..].
- When the [Select Backup Drive] window opens, **[Clk]**[OK] to accept the default file and drive. If your computer has two floppy drives, and you are not using drive A:, select a drive from the drop-down list before you **[Clk]**[OK].
- Quicken will confirm that the back-up has been successful: **[Clk]**[OK].
- On the first occasion make a second back-up; alternate between the two sets as you back up your work.
- Should you suffer a loss of data from your hard disk, first reinstall Quicken, then from the [File] menu choose [File Operations] followed by [Restore..].

New Files

- If you decide to keep your home finances on Quicken as well as your business accounts, you will probably wish to keep them on separate files.
- Open the [File] menu and choose [New..]. **[Clk]**[OK] to continue.
- In the [Create Quicken File] window give your file a name, being careful not to change the QDT extension, select the drive and directory where your file will be stored and choose the standard categories you want. **[Clk]**[OK].
- Quicken always starts with the last file used; to select an alternative press **[Ctrl+O]** and choose your file at the [Open Quicken File] window.

Passwords

- You may wish to set a password to protect your business file from interference. Open the file that you wish to protect and from the [File] menu choose [Passwords] and [File]. Type your password at the [Set Up Password] window and **[Clk]**[OK]; confirm the password by entering it again, then **[Clk]**[OK]. Quicken will ask for a password before opening this file.
- If you choose [Transaction] from the [Password] options, you can then enter the date of the last transaction you wish to protect from alteration, so that there is no need to close files at the end of the year.

42

File Management

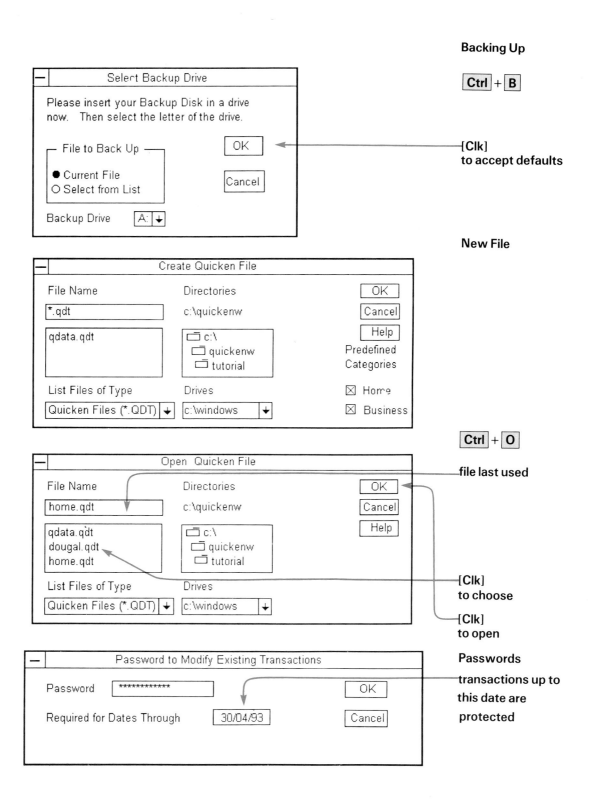

Backing Up

`Ctrl` + `B`

Select Backup Drive

Please insert your Backup Disk in a drive now.   Then select the letter of the drive.

┌─ File to Back Up ─┐

● Current File
○ Select from List

OK

Cancel

Backup Drive   `A:` ▾

[Clk]
to accept defaults

New File

Create Quicken File

File Name   Directories   OK

*.qdt   c:\quickenw   Cancel

qdata.qdt   📁 c:\   Help
                          📁 quickenw   Predefined
                          📁 tutorial   Categories

List Files of Type   Drives   ☒ Home
Quicken Files (*.QDT) ▾ c:\windows ▾   ☒ Business

`Ctrl` + `O`

Open Quicken File

File Name   Directories   OK ◄──── file last used

home.qdt   c:\quickenw   Cancel

qdata.qdt   📁 c:\   Help
dougal.qdt   📁 quickenw
home.qdt   📁 tutorial

List Files of Type   Drives   [Clk]
Quicken Files (*.QDT) ▾ c:\windows ▾   to choose

                                                      [Clk]
                                                      to open

---

Passwords

Password to Modify Existing Transactions

Password   ***********   OK

Required for Dates Through   30/04/93   Cancel

transactions up to
this date are
protected

43

The Icon Bar

The icon bar, containing the most commonly used menu items, has been used wherever possible in the early pages of this guide. It provides an equivalent for Mouse users of the keyboard shortcut. Furthermore, it can be modified to suit your particular needs.

Instructions

- To remove the icons and display only text in the icon bar, **[Clk]** the [Iconbar] button and **[Clk]** the [Display Icons] checkbox in the [Customise Iconbar] window to remove the check. Your display will now resemble that used in the illustration pages, freeing a little extra space if you like to stretch the transaction register to the limit.
- If you find that you make little use of an icon, but need the space for something else, delete it: **[Drag]** the scroll box until the icon you wish to delete appears, **[Clk]** to select it, **[Clk]** the [Delete] button and **[Clk]** [OK] when asked to confirm.
- The [Use Acct] and [Use Tx] icons at the right end of the bar are available if you use an account other than the current account register regularly. **[Clk]** [Use Acct]; **[Clk]** [OK] to continue when you have read the information.
- At the [Assign Account to Icon] window, **[Drag]** the scroll box until [Visa] is visible; **[Clk]** to make [Visa] the [Account to Load]. You can have it loaded at the transaction entry stage, or at the reconcile stage. **[Clk]** [OK] to set up. When you **[Clk]** the [Use Acct] icon, the [Credit Card: Visa] transaction register will be displayed.
- To change to a more descriptive icon, **[Clk]** [Iconbar]: at the [Customise Iconbar] window select [Use Acct]; **[Clk]** [Edit].
- At the [Edit Action on Iconbar] window, [Use an Account] will be selected; **[Clk]** [Change]. Scroll through the [Graphics] in the [Change Iconbar Item] window until you find an appropriate icon. **[Clk]** on your choice to select it, then **[Clk]** [OK]. You can also change the text at this window.
- To add a new icon to the icon bar, **[Clk]** [Iconbar] then [Add New] at the [Customise Iconbar] window. The [Add Action to Iconbar] window is similar to the [Edit Action] window used in the previous paragraph. **[Clk]** [File Backup..] to select it as the [Icon Action] if it is not pre-selected, **[Clk]** [OK] and the graphic will appear in the box (there are no alternatives). **[Clk]** [OK] and the [Assign File Backup to Icon] window will offer you the opportunity to skip the initial dialogue.
- **[Clk]** [OK] and the Backup icon will be added to the icon bar.

Helpful tips

The Backup icon is particularly worth adding to your screen display because the Windows version of Quicken does not have the [Set Backup Frequency] with automatic reminder which the DOS version possessed.

Backup needs no "Speed key", as the shortcut **[Ctrl+B]** already exists. If you use classes, it is worth adding a Class List icon to the bar.

The Icon Bar

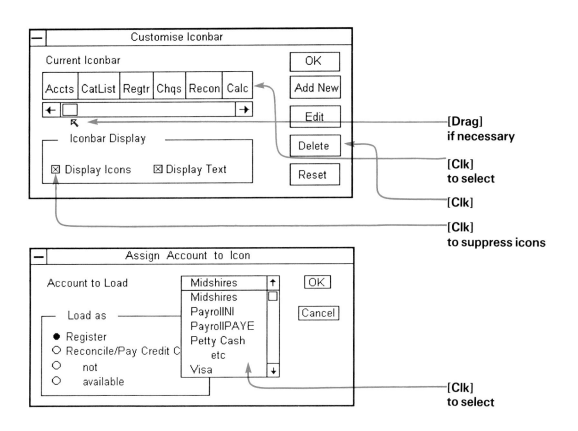

Customise Iconbar

Current Iconbar

| Accts | CatList | Regtr | Chqs | Recon | Calc |

Iconbar Display

☒ Display Icons   ☒ Display Text

OK

Add New

Edit — [Drag] if necessary

Delete — [Clk] to select

Reset — [Clk]

— [Clk] to suppress icons

Assign Account to Icon

Account to Load

Midshires
Midshires
PayrollNI
PayrollPAYE
Petty Cash
    etc
Visa

OK

Cancel

Load as

● Register
○ Reconcile/Pay Credit C
○   not
○   available

— [Clk] to select

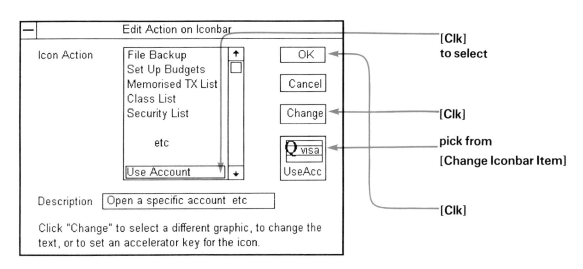

Edit Action on Iconbar

Icon Action

File Backup
Set Up Budgets
Memorised TX List
Class List
Security List

etc

Use Account

OK — [Clk] to select

Cancel

Change — [Clk]

UseAcc — pick from [Change Iconbar Item]

— [Clk]

Description   Open a specific account etc

Click "Change" to select a different graphic, to change the text, or to set an accelerator key for the icon.

QuickInvoice 1

Purchasers of QuickInvoice for Windows are able to create and print invoices, then send the data from the invoices to Quicken to be incorporated in a specified asset account. Invoice forms are available from Intuit, but if your prefer to use blank paper, this must be A4 (210mm by 297mm).

Minimum Hardware Requirements

An IBM 286 or compatible computer with 3MB RAM is required; the hard disk must have 1.25MB of available space in addition to the 3MB required by Quicken. Quicken 2 for Windows must already be installed.

Installation

● The installation process follows that described in Getting Started; it is essential that QuickInvoice is placed in the same directory as Quicken. If you used Express Installation this is "quickenw" – C:\quickenw – which is the default in QuickInvoice's Express Installation.

● To run QuickInvoice, **[Dbl-Clk]** on the Quicken group icon, then **[Dbl-Clk]** on the QuickInvoice program icon to start both QuickInvoice and Quicken. You may also start Quicken in the usual way and select QuickInvoice from the **[Activities]** menu when you need it.

Setting Up

When you start QuickInvoice a blank invoice is displayed, but on the first occasion this has in front of it the [Set Up Company] window. Before you can write and print invoices you need to enter some basic information about your business and its accounts.

● If your business is not registered for VAT, **[Clk]** the [Include VAT on invoice] box to deselect it; type ⟨**0**⟩ (zero) in the [Tax Rate] field.

● The Asset Account "Credit Sales" was created in section 17 Credit Sales and should be used here. **[Clk]** the Arrow to see the drop-down list, then **[Clk]** [Credit Sales] to select it.

● The Cash Account "Undeposited Pmt" is used to hold customer payments, including those made in advance or at the time of sale and listed on invoices, until you deposit them in your bank account and record the transaction as a transfer. This process makes bank reconciliation a little easier.

Writing Invoices

● The [Customer Name of ID] field should be used to set up a reference or code for your regular customers. For subsequent invoices, selecting the code from the drop-down list will cause QuickInvoice to fill in the [Name and Address] field.

● The [Item Code] field ensures that invoice entries are assigned to the correct Quicken category or sub category. **[Clk]** [Record] when you have entered details of the invoice.

● To create Item Codes, **[Clk]** the **[Lists]** menu and select [Item] then [New]. Complctc thc [Sct Up Item] window and **[Clk]** [OK] when done.

QuickInvoice 1

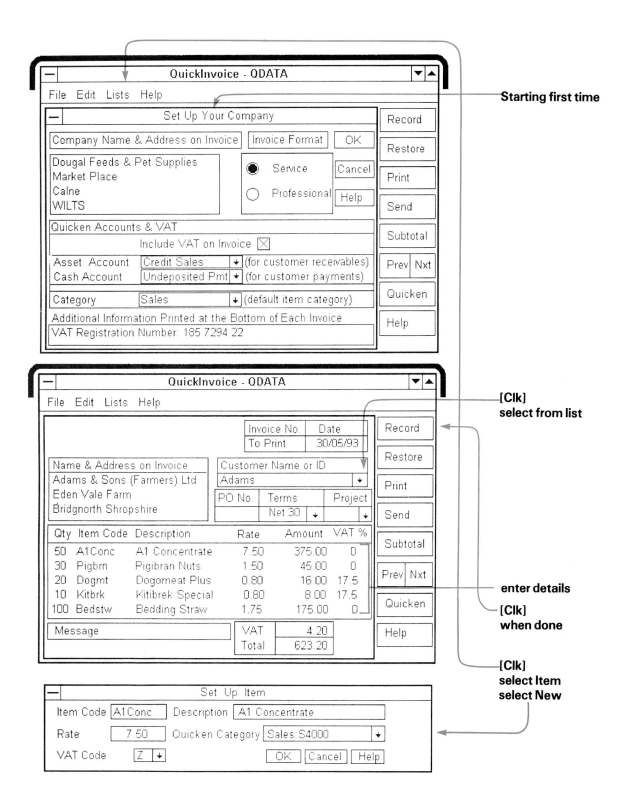

Starting first time

QuickInvoice - QDATA

File   Edit   Lists   Help

Set Up Your Company

| Company Name & Address on Invoice | Invoice Format | OK |

Dougal Feeds & Pet Supplies
Market Place
Calne
WILTS

⦿ Service   Cancel
◯ Professional   Help

Quicken Accounts & VAT

Include VAT on Invoice ☒

| Asset   Account | Credit Sales | ↓ | (for customer receivables) |
| Cash Account | Undeposited Pmt | ↓ | (for customer payments) |

| Category | Sales | ↓ | (default item category) |

Additional Information Printed at the Bottom of Each Invoice
VAT Registration Number: 185 7294 22

Record
Restore
Print
Send
Subtotal
Prev | Nxt
Quicken
Help

**[Clk]
select from list**

QuickInvoice - QDATA

File   Edit   Lists   Help

| | Invoice No. | Date |
| | To Print | 30/05/93 |

Name & Address on Invoice	Customer Name or ID
Adams & Sons (Farmers) Ltd	Adams	↓
Eden Vale Farm	PO No.	Terms	Project
Bridgnorth Shropshire		Net 30 ↓	↓

Qty	Item Code	Description	Rate	Amount	VAT %
50	A1Conc	A1 Concentrate	7.50	375.00	0
30	Pigbrn	Pigibran Nuts	1.50	45.00	0
20	Dogmt	Dogomeat Plus	0.80	16.00	17.5
10	Kitbrk	Kitibrek Special	0.80	8.00	17.5
100	Bedstw	Bedding Straw	1.75	175.00	0

| Message | VAT | 4.20 |
| | Total | 623.20 |

Record
Restore
Print
Send
Subtotal
Prev | Nxt
Quicken
Help

**enter details
[Clk]
when done**

**[Clk]
select Item
select New**

Set Up Item

Item Code	A1Conc	Description	A1 Concentrate
Rate	7.50	Quicken Category	Sales:S4000	↓
VAT Code	Z ↓		OK	Cancel	Help

QuickInvoice Contd.

Once you have created and recorded an invoice, it may be printed and sent to Quicken. An invoice cannot be altered after it has been sent; the transaction and the invoice must be deleted, and a new invoice written and sent.

Instructions

- Check your printer set up: from the [File] menu choose [Printer Setup]. If you use plain paper or letterhead paper for your invoices there should be no need to adjust the alignment. If you use continuous preprinted forms, print a sample and, if necessary, correct vertical alignment as described in section 11, Printing Cheques. After printing, **[Clk]** [OK].
- **[Clk]** the [Send] button to send the invoice data to Quicken. In the [Select Invoices to Send] window are all the invoices except those voided or already sent. **[Clk]** [Send]. The invoices will be marked and shaded to show that they cannot now be altered.
- Leave QuickInvoice and switch to Quicken. **[Clk]** [Quicken] at the [Write Invoices] window and open the [Credit Sales] transaction register where you will find each invoice entered, with details of each item on the invoice displayed in the [Splits] window.
- When you receive a cheque from a customer, make the necessary entries in the [Credit Sales] transaction register, being careful to use the [Customer Name or ID] from your QuickInvoice customer list in the [Payee] field, and remembering to **[Dbl-Clk]** in the [Clr] field.
- Find the invoice to which the cheque relates, and if payment in full has been made, mark the [Clr] field. **[Clk]** [Record] to complete the process.

Helpful tips

From time to time you should remove paid invoices from your QuickInvoice file. Print out your Quicken [Credit Sales] register. Switch to QuickInvoice. Open the QuickInvoice [Edit] menu; select [Delete Invoices]. Invoices which have been printed and sent are marked "Delete" in the [Select Invoices to Delete] window. Select invoices which are not marked with an asterisk in the [Clr] field of the [Credit Sales] register to indicate payment in full, and **[Clk]** the [Mark] button to make the [Delete] field blank. **[Clk]** [Delete].

Invoices are automatically memorised, and will be recalled automatically from a [Memorised Invoice] list.

To customise QuickInvoice, open the [Edit] menu and choose [Preferences].

To exit from QuickInvoice open the [File] menu and choose [Exit QuickInvoice]; then exit from Quicken.

If you are working in Quicken, exiting from that program also closes QuickInvoice.

QuickInvoice Contd.

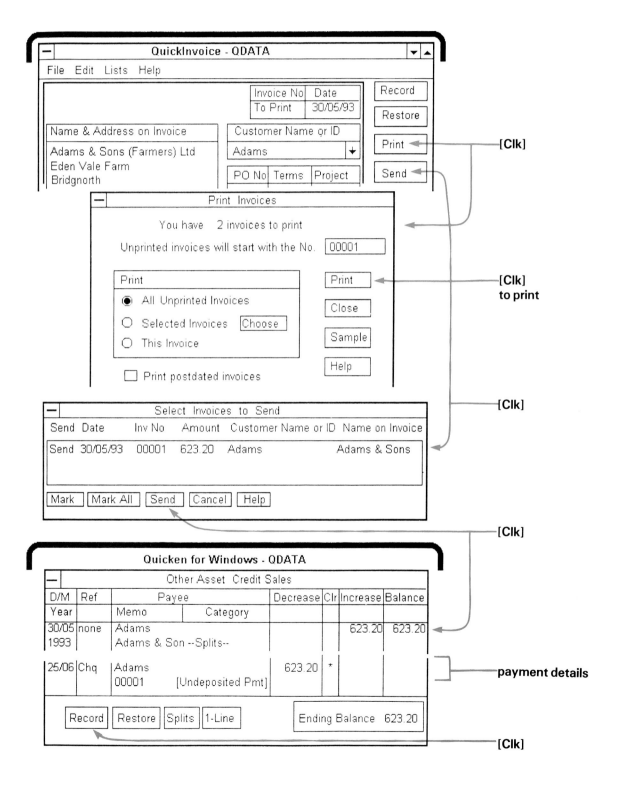

Introduction

The DOS version of Quicken was introduced to the UK market in the autumn of 1992, and although it was soon followed by a Windows version, there are, no doubt, many satisfied DOS users, for, though the opportunity was taken to add some new features to Quicken, the DOS version remains an excellent product almost as easy to use as the Windows version, and much more modest in its hardware requirements.

Minimum Hardware Requirements

Quicken for DOS requires an IBM PC or a PC-compatible computer with 512K of installed memory, one floppy drive and a hard disk drive. The operating system must be DOS 2.0 or higher.

Seeking Help

Ease of use is one of Quicken's strengths, and on screen help is readily available. At any Quicken screen, menu or window where you need support, press **[F1]**. Press **[F1]** again to see the Help Table of Contents. Press **[Ctrl+F1]** hold down the Control key while you press **[F1]** to consult the Help Index. There are two levels of index, use the **[+]** and **[−]** keys to toggle between them.

Conventions

Throughout this guide, the following conventions have been used:

⏎	press the Enter key.
[F1]	press the key named in the box.
[Lt] [Rt] [Up] [Dn]	refer to the Direction (Arrow) keys.
⟨**..words..**⟩	type the words between ⟨...⟩.
[Edit] menu	menus and menu items are bold.
[Date]	other options.

Mouse users will probably prefer to use their mouse: the RIGHT button is **[Esc]**: all other operations are carried out by clicking the LEFT button once, or in some instances, twice.

To use this guide, simply follow the step by step instructions: these are supplemented by the illustrations. The DOS portion covers the basics of preparing to use Quicken UK version 6 for DOS, after which you can switch to the main body of the guide and work through the examples. You will soon realise that the major difference is in the Windows bias towards the Mouse when making choices – "point and click"; data entry is little changed.

Towards the end of this section there is a comparison of some popular DOS and Windows screens to help you make the best use of the main part of this guide. It is hoped that when you reach the end you will be familiar with the basic principles of Quicken, ready to apply them to your own circumstances and ready to try out other processes – use the Sample file or the Dougal file first!

Introduction

At a work screen or menu F1

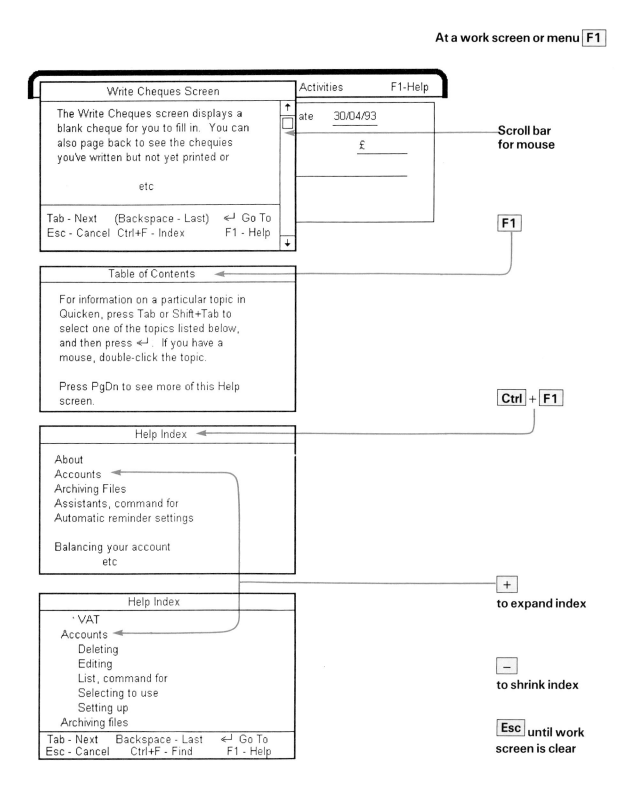

Write Cheques Screen	Activities F1-Help

The Write Cheques screen displays a blank cheque for you to fill in. You can also page back to see the chequies you've written but not yet printed or

etc

Tab - Next   (Backspace - Last)   ↵ Go To
Esc - Cancel Ctrl+F - Index   F1 - Help

ate   30/04/93

£

Scroll bar for mouse

F1

Table of Contents

For information on a particular topic in Quicken, press Tab or Shift+Tab to select one of the topics listed below, and then press ↵. If you have a mouse, double-click the topic.

Press PgDn to see more of this Help screen.

Ctrl + F1

Help Index

About
Accounts
Archiving Files
Assistants, command for
Automatic reminder settings

Balancing your account
        etc

Help Index

· VAT
Accounts
    Deleting
    Editing
    List, command for
    Selecting to use
    Setting up
Archiving files

Tab - Next   Backspace - Last   ↵ Go To
Esc - Cancel   Ctrl+F - Find   F1 - Help

\+
to expand index

\−
to shrink index

Esc until work
screen is clear

51

Getting Started

Before you can use the program, it must be installed to suit your equipment. This task is particularly easy with Quicken. It is prudent to copy the master disks before installing the program.

Instructions

- Be sure you have sufficient blank, formatted disks on which to make copies of your Quicken master disks.
- Switch on your computer, and when the system prompt C:⟩ appears, place a master disk in the floppy drive, type ⟨**diskcopy**⟩ and press the **Enter** key – or the **Return** key, which is marked with a ⎰←⎱.
- Follow the instructions which appear on screen and change disks when required. Carefully label the copy you have made.
- Repeat the process until you have copied all the Quicken master disks, which should then be stored in a safe place.
- If you have two floppy drives, you may use the DOS "copy" command. Place a master disk in drive A, a blank, formatted disk in drive B, and at the system prompt type ⟨**copy a:*.* b:**⟩ (the space before b: is essential) and then press ⎰←⎱.
- When copying is complete, place your copy of Quicken Disk 1 – the Install Disk – in drive A. If your screen does not display the A:⟩ prompt, type ⟨**a:**⟩ and press ⎰←⎱.
- At the A:⟩ prompt, type ⟨**install**⟩ and press ⎰←⎱.
- Follow the instructions that the Install program displays on your screen.
- To run Quicken after installation, at the C:⟩ prompt simply type ⟨**Q**⟩ and press ⎰←⎱.
- On first use the Welcome screen appears: press ⎰←⎱ to see the 10 minute Overview.
- On subsequent use, the Main Menu appears. If you wish to see the Overview again, select **[Use Tutorials/Assistants]** from the Main Menu.

Helpful tips

If your printer is not among those listed, refer to your printer manual; most printers emulate one or more of the models produced by the major manufacturers. Select one of those that your printer emulates.

"Billminder" checks your Quicken data whenever you switch on your computer and reminds you if there is any action overdue, or almost due. It is well worth selecting Billminder at installation.

Always leave Quicken by selecting **[Exit]** from the Main Menu.

Getting Started

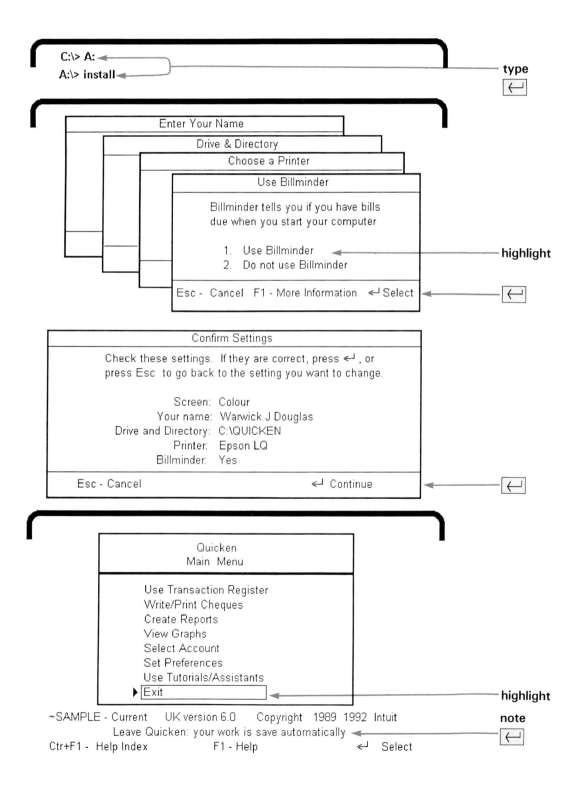

C:\> A: **type**

A:\> install   ⏎

Enter Your Name

Drive & Directory

Choose a Printer

Use Billminder

Billminder tells you if you have bills
due when you start your computer

1. Use Billminder   ← **highlight**
2. Do not use Billminder

Esc - Cancel   F1 - More Information   ⏎ Select   ← ⏎

Confirm Settings

Check these settings. If they are correct, press ⏎ , or
press Esc to go back to the setting you want to change.

Screen: Colour
Your name: Warwick J Douglas
Drive and Directory: C:\QUICKEN
Printer: Epson LQ
Billminder: Yes

Esc - Cancel   ⏎ Continue   ← ⏎

Quicken
Main Menu

Use Transaction Register
Write/Print Cheques
Create Reports
View Graphs
Select Account
Set Preferences
Use Tutorials/Assistants
▶ Exit   ← **highlight**

~SAMPLE - Current   UK version 6.0   Copyright   1989 1992 Intuit   **note**
Leave Quicken: your work is save automatically ←   ⏎
Ctr+F1 - Help Index   F1 - Help   ⏎   Select

53

Menus & Preferences

Quicken menus are easy to use and a prompt line at the foot of the screen gives a brief description of the activities available in the item currently highlighted by the selection bar. You may select an item either by moving the selection bar with the **[Up]** or **[Dn]** keys and then pressing ⏎, or by pressing the highlighted letter in the item.

Many Quicken work screens have pulldown menus – listed in the menu bar at the top of your screen. To open one of these menus, hold down the **[Alt]** key while pressing the letter highlighted in the menu title: **[Alt+E]**, for example, opens the **[Edit]** menu.

Before you begin work with Quicken, you may wish to set your printer to the way you wish it to print cheques and reports.

Instructions

- At the Main Menu, use the **[Dn]** key to move the selection bar highlight to **[Set Preferences]** and press ⏎. The new menu will be over the Main Menu.
- Press **[P]** to select **[Printer Settings]**, then **[C]** to choose **[Settings for Printing Cheques]**.
- You should see displayed the name of the printer you installed and the current style – the number of characters per inch, draft or letter quality, paper size.
- The range of **[Available Styles]** depends on your printer's capability. Move the selection high-light to the style you wish to use and press ⏎.
- If you use standard continuous fan-fold paper, which is 11″ long, you will need to alter the [Lines per page] in the **[Settings for Printing Reports]**.
- From the **[Set Preferences]** menu, press **[P]** then **[R]** to move to **[Report Printer Settings]**.
- Move the highlight to, say [17cpi,NLQ,Ltr] and press ⏎. This will produce condensed print on US Letter size paper, which is 11″ long, The [Lines per page] will now show [66].

Helpful tips

[Lines per page] is only relevant when adjusting cheque printer settings if you use a laser printer, when it should be set to 63.

If you wish to have readily available a second style for reports, select **[Alternate Settings for Reports]** from the **[Printer Settings]** menu.

You can return to the Main Menu from whatever you may be doing by pressing **[Esc]** until the Main Menu reappears.

Menus & Preferences

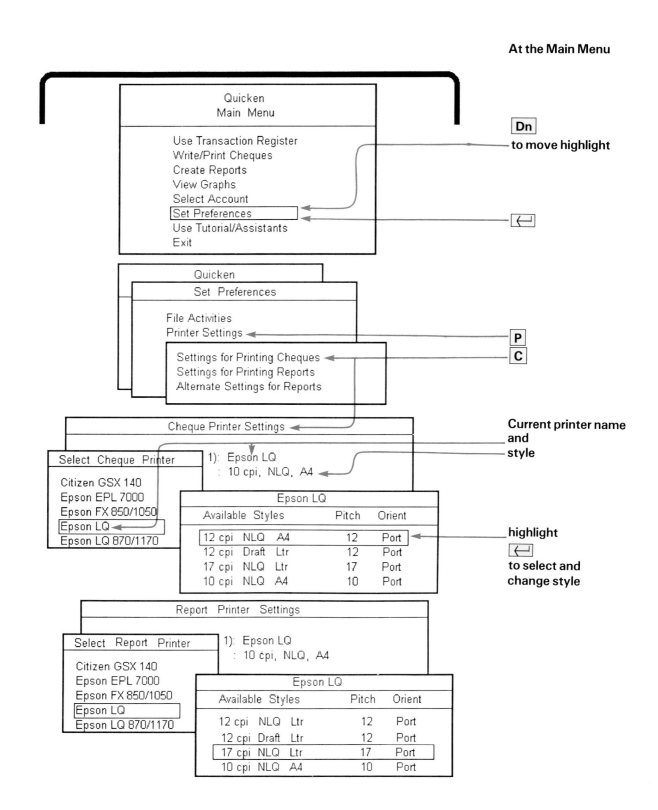

```
                    Quicken
                   Main Menu

            Use Transaction Register
            Write/Print Cheques
            Create Reports
            View Graphs
            Select Account
           [Set Preferences          ]
            Use Tutorial/Assistants
            Exit
```

Dn
to move highlight

↵

```
                    Quicken
                 Set Preferences

            File Activities
            Printer Settings

           Settings for Printing Cheques
           Settings for Printing Reports
           Alternate Settings for Reports
```

P

C

```
          Cheque Printer Settings

Select  Cheque  Printer     1):  Epson LQ
                              :  10 cpi, NLQ, A4
Citizen GSX 140
Epson EPL 7000
Epson FX 850/1050
[Epson LQ        ]
Epson LQ 870/1170
```

Current printer name and style

```
                   Epson LQ

Available  Styles          Pitch    Orient

[12 cpi  NLQ   A4           12      Port ]
 12 cpi  Draft Ltr          12      Port
 17 cpi  NLQ   Ltr          17      Port
 10 cpi  NLQ   A4           10      Port
```

highlight

↵

to select and change style

```
          Report  Printer  Settings

Select  Report  Printer     1):  Epson LQ
                              :  10 cpi, NLQ, A4
Citizen GSX 140
Epson EPL 7000
Epson FX 850/1050
[Epson LQ        ]
Epson LQ 870/1170
```

```
                   Epson LQ

Available  Styles          Pitch    Orient

 12 cpi  NLQ   Ltr          12      Port
 12 cpi  Draft Ltr          12      Port
[17 cpi  NLQ   Ltr          17      Port ]
 10 cpi  NLQ   A4           10      Port
```

55

Setting Up

After completing the "Quick Tour" using the Sample file, you should set up a new file to use with this guide. Later you will need to create a Quicken file to hold all the accounts relating to your business, and, if you wish, another file to manage your personal finances. To begin, however, you need one file and at least one account.

Instructions

- At the Main Menu, press **[P]** for **[Set Preferences]**. **[F]** for **[File Activities]** and **[S]** to **[Select/Set Up File]**. The existing file SAMPLE should be highlighted in the [Select/Set Up File] box.
- Press **[Up]** to move the selection highlight to **[Set Up File]** and press ⏎ to continue.
- In the [Set Up File] window type the file name ⟨**dougal**⟩ and **[Tab]**. **[Tab]** again to accept the location offered.
- Press ⏎ to go on to select standard categories under which your income and expenses will be classified. Press **[2]** to choose **[Business Categories]** at the [Select Standard Categories] window.
- Press ⏎ to continue, and the **[Select/Set Up File]** box should include your newly created file. Move the highlight to select it and press ⏎.
- Press ⏎ to choose **[New Account]** from the [Select Account to Use] box.
- **[Tab]** to accept [Account Type: 1]; type the name of the bank, **[Tab]** to [Balance:] and enter the amount, then the date from which your accounts will be kept in Quicken, and, if required, a description. **[Tab]** to accept [Currency] then press ⏎.

Helpful tips

It is simpler to keep all files in one drive and directory, so there should be no need to alter the location. If you wish to store your data on a floppy disk, refer to the Miscellany section at the end of this guide.

Press **[F1]** in the [Set Up File] box to see the rules for naming files.

You may adapt the standard list of categories to suit your needs by deleting from or adding to the list: if you wish to create your own categories from the start, select [4. Neither] at the [Select Standard Categories] window.

The **[Tutorials and Assistants]** menu will also help you to set up a new file and a new account.

Balances used in setting up new accounts are opening balances, and must have been reconciled with control accounts or bank statements.

Setting Up

At the Main Menu P

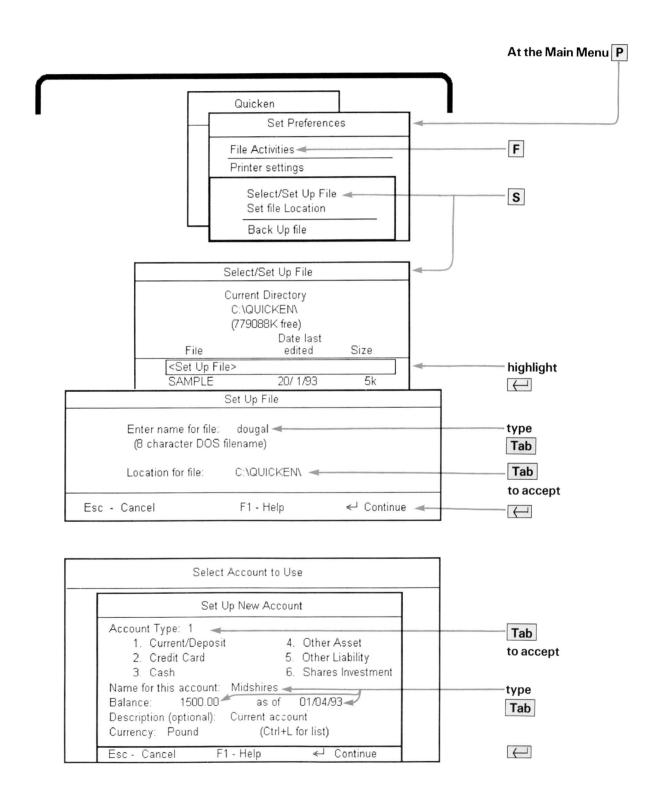

Organising

Many users will find the standard categories meet most of their needs, though they may wish to modify the list: a simple change of name or description might suffice. But you may wish to add new categories, or delete a category from the standard list; or you may wish to divide a category into sub-categories. These operations may be carried out at any time, though it is better to have come to Quicken with a clear notion of how you wish to organise your accounts.

Instructions

- To see the standard list of categories, at the Main Menu press **[R]** for **[Transaction Register]**, **[Alt+S]** for the **[Shortcuts]** menu and **[C]** for the **[Category & Transfer List]**. To see the remainder of the list, press **[PgDn]**.

Adding or Deleting Categories

- Move the selection highlight to the category you wish to delete – for example [Rental Income] – and press **[Ctrl+D]**. A warning will appear, press ⏎ to confirm and complete the deletion.
- To add to the list, move the selection highlight to [New Category] and press ⏎ to reveal the [Set Up New Category] box.
- Type ⟨**Payroll**⟩ and press **[Tab]**. Press **[E]** to specify [Expense] as the category type, then **[Tab]** to the [Description] field. Type ⟨**Wages & Salaries**⟩, then **[Tab]** to [Tax-related] and press **[Y]**.
- **[Tab]** to the [Usual VAT Code] field: press **[F7]** to see the [VAT Table]. You will be asked if you want the usual VAT settings; ⏎ to accept.
- Check the table for the "Exempt" code; press **[Esc]** to clear the screen and type ⟨**E**⟩. To set up the new category, press ⏎.

To Add Subcategories

- Move the selection bar to the category you wish to provide with subcategories and press **[Ctrl+Ins]**. The [Set Up Category] screen will appear, with the category type already shown as [S] – subcategory.
- Enter the details as shown in the third illustration on the facing page. Repeat the process, setting up subcategories S4001, Petfoods; S4002, Veterinary Supplies; and S4005, Other Sales. As subcategories of Purchases, create P5000, P5001, P5002 and P5005.
- You may subdivide sub categories – this is particularly useful if you sell VAT and non-VAT products under, say, Other Sales – by pressing **[Ctrl+Ins]** on the subcategory to be divided. The final outcome would resemble the fourth illustration.

Helpful tip

The category name [Payroll] is obligatory if you intend to use Quicken to carry out payroll tasks.
The brackets on the final item in the [Category & Transfer List] indicate that [Midshires] is an account, not a category.

Organising

At the Main Menu R for [Transaction Register]

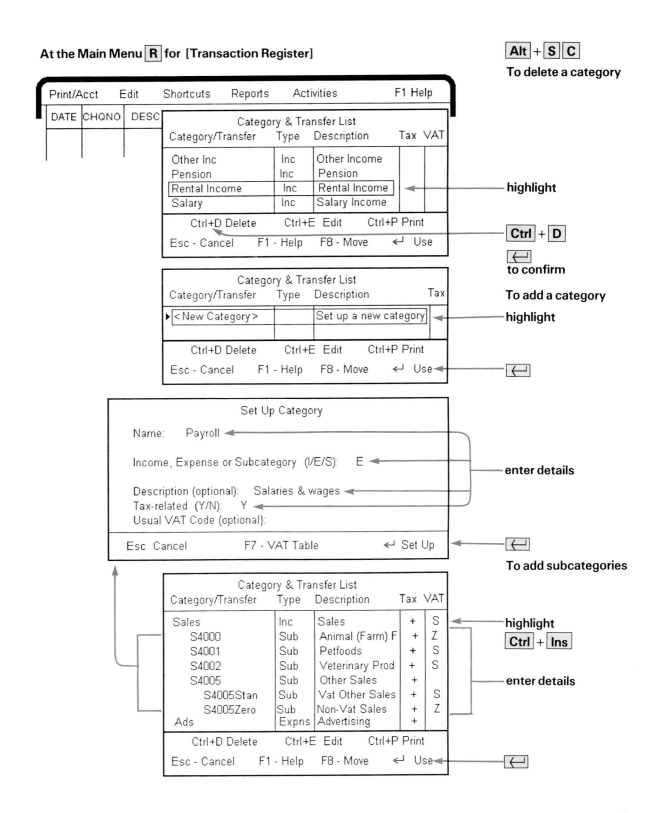

Alt + S C
To delete a category

highlight

Ctrl + D
←
to confirm

To add a category
highlight

←

enter details

←

To add subcategories

highlight
Ctrl + Ins

enter details

←

59

DOS and Windows

Users of Quicken for DOS will find that the transition to the main section of this manual, or equally, the transition to Quicken for Windows is not difficult. Apart from the "point and click" approach characteristic of Windows software, and the associated buttons and check boxes, the appearance of the main area of the screen is reassuringly familiar; data entry is made easier, but account registers are basically unchanged, as might be expected, and lists (whether category, account or class) only slightly altered.

The illustration page compares the [Set Up Category] and the [Report Options] screens.

Set Up Category

The layout is similar and the main difference in entering information is that the keyboard is used to replace the default values in the DOS program, while Windows uses the button or check box. The drop-down list of categories to be used when setting up subcategories in the Windows version might be thought clumsier than first selecting the category you wish to provide a subcategory for, pressing **[Ctrl+Ins]** and then filling in the details.

Report Options

There is a much greater use of drop-down lists, but the options are similar: changes are minor – as shown in the illustration, where "External Transfers Only" (DOS) becomes "Exclude Internal".

Quick Keys & Keyboard Shortcuts

The Windows version retains most of the keyboard shortcuts used in the DOS version.

DOS & Windows

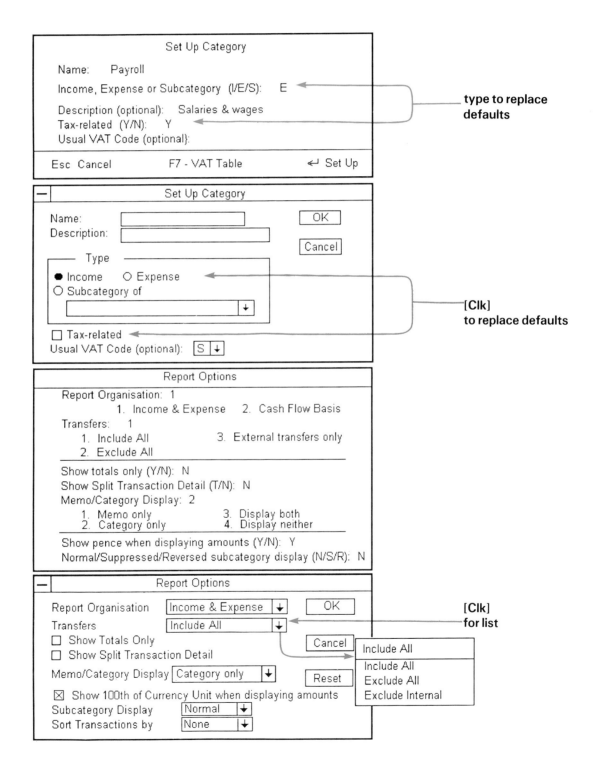

Set Up Category

Name: Payroll

Income, Expense or Subcategory (I/E/S):   E ◄─────────────────────┐
                                                                      ├── **type to replace defaults**
Description (optional):   Salaries & wages
Tax-related (Y/N):   Y ◄──┘
Usual VAT Code (optional):

Esc Cancel   F7 - VAT Table   ↵ Set Up

Set Up Category

Name: [   ]   [OK]
Description: [   ]
                                             [Cancel]
    ┌─ Type ──────────────────────────────┐
    │ ● Income   ○ Expense ◄────────────┼──┐
    │ ○ Subcategory of   │ ├── **[Clk]**
    │   [   ] ↓   │ │   **to replace defaults**
    ├──────────────────────────────────────┤ │
    │ □ Tax-related ◄─────────────────────┼──┘
    Usual VAT Code (optional): [S ↓]

Report Options

Report Organisation: 1
            1. Income & Expense   2. Cash Flow Basis
Transfers: 1
        1. Include All   3. External transfers only
        2. Exclude All

Show totals only (Y/N): N
Show Split Transaction Detail (T/N): N
Memo/Category Display: 2
        1. Memo only   3. Display both
        2. Category only   4. Display neither

Show pence when displaying amounts (Y/N): Y
Normal/Suppressed/Reversed subcategory display (N/S/R): N

Report Options

Report Organisation [Income & Expense ↓]   [OK]   **[Clk]**
                                                             for list
Transfers   [Include All   ↓] ◄──────┐
□ Show Totals Only   [Cancel]   │   ┌──────────────────┐
□ Show Split Transaction Detail   └──►│ Include All   │
                                                         ├──────────────────┤
Memo/Category Display [Category only ↓]   [Reset]   │ Include All   │
                                                         │ Exclude All   │
⊠ Show 100th of Currency Unit when displaying amounts   │ Exclude Internal │
Subcategory Display   [Normal ↓]   └──────────────────┘
Sort Transactions by [None   ↓]

61

Miscellany

Backing Up & Restoring

When you leave Quicken and return to the C:> prompt, there is a reminder to back up your data. You should back up your Quicken files regularly – at least once a week – and set the Back Up Reminder so that this important matter is not overlooked.

Instructions

- At the Main Menu select **[Set Preferences]**, **[File Activities]** and **[Set Backup Frequency]**.
- Enter **[2]** in the [Frequency] field: you will be reminded to back up each time you use Quicken.
- At a Transaction Register pull down the **[Print/Acct]** menu and select **[Backup File]**. Follow the instructions on screen. From the Main Menu you can back up using **[Ctrl+B]** or **[Ctrl+E]** – to back up and exit.
- If you have more than one Quicken file you must set the Back Up Reminder for each file separately.
- Should you suffer a disaster with your hard disk, first reinstall Quicken, then start from the Main Menu and select in turn **[Set Preferences]**, **[File Activities]** and **[Restore File]**. You will be asked which drive Quicken is to restore from; then follow the on screen instructions.

Keeping Data on a Floppy Disk

Many users prefer to keep data on floppy disks; if you wish to do this it is necessary to tell Quicken where to find its data. You can still set the Back Up Reminder, but backing up will be done by copying the floppy. Press **[Esc]** to cancel the message.

Instructions

- At the Main Menu choose **[Set Preferences]**, **[File Activities]** and **[Set File Location]**. Type the new path name, which will be a floppy drive: – ⟨**A:**⟩, for example.
- To copy the file, select **[Copy File]** from the **[File Activities]** menu. Complete the entries in the [Copy File] window.
- If you have just one floppy drive, specify that you wish to copy to a different disk: Quicken will tell you when to change disks.
- Note that you can set a date range in the [Copy File] window.

Password Protection

While you have been using this guide it has not mattered very much if you found yourself entering transactions in the SAMPLE file provided with the program, and it is recommended that you continue to use these files to try out customised reports and other more advanced uses.

To make sure that your business file is not interfered with, you may wish to set a file password.

Instructions

- From the Main Menu select **[Set Preferences]**, **[Password Settings]** and **[File Password]**. Your password can have up to 16 characters. You have to type the password a second time to confirm it, then press ⏎.
- Set a **[Transaction Password]** to close an accounting period without using the "Archive" or "Start New Year" procedures. The date you specify is the last date for which the password must be given.

Windows and DOS

You can set up Quicken to run from the Windows 3.0 or 3.1 desktop, but you must never run a DOS based back up program under Windows, and it is all too easy to forget, if you have been using Quicken on a full screen for some time, that you are not in DOS.

Windows users running Quicken for DOS should, therefore, run Quicken from DOS and not from the desktop.

Opening Balances

When you begin bookkeeping on Quicken it is possible that you may have some outstanding accounts receivable or payable. These should be brought in from your previous records. Enter the transactions in the register as you would enter current transactions: invoices outstanding are entered under the date payment is due, and cheques for your creditors are post-dated.

If the invoices are long outstanding, use the first available date as the due date.

FINALLY, whichever version you have, don't forget to complete and post your Quicken registration card.